STORY OF
TAN

THE HISTORY OF
TARTAN

The evocative story of the famous cloth of Scotland, and of
the myths, legends and stirring history that are woven through
it, with over 250 colour photographs and fine art images

IAIN ZACZEK

southwater

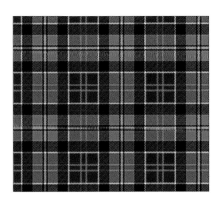

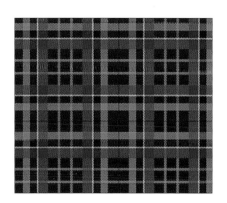

This edition is published by Southwater

Southwater is an imprint of Anness Publishing Ltd
Hermes House, 88–89 Blackfriars Road, London SE1 8HA
tel. 020 7401 2077; fax 020 7633 9499
www.southwaterbooks.com; info@anness.com

© Anness Publishing Ltd 2005

UK agent: The Manning Partnership Ltd
6 The Old Dairy, Melcombe Road, Bath BA2 3LR
tel. 01225 478444; fax 01225 478440
sales@manning-partnership.co.uk

UK distributor: Grantham Book Services Ltd
Isaac Newton Way, Alma Park Industrial Estate
Grantham, Lincs NG31 9SD
tel. 01476 541080; fax 01476 541061
orders@gbs.tbs-ltd.co.uk

North American agent/distributor: National Book Network
4501 Forbes Boulevard, Suite 200, Lanham, MD 20706
tel. 301 459 3366; fax 301 429 5746; www.nbnbooks.com

Australian agent/distributor: Pan Macmillan Australia
Level 18, St Martins Tower, 31 Market St, Sydney, NSW 2000
tel. 1300 135 113; fax 1300 135 103
customer.service@macmillan.com.au

New Zealand agent/distributor: David Bateman Ltd
30 Tarndale Grove, Off Bush Road, Albany, Auckland
tel. (09) 415 7664; fax (09) 415 8892

Previously published as part of a larger volume,
The Illustrated Encyclopedia of Tartan

Publisher: Joanna Lorenz
Editorial Director: Helen Sudell
Editors: Joanne Rippin and Elizabeth Woodland
Picture Research: Bob Lawson
Editorial Reader: Penelope Goodare
Designer: Nigel Partridge
Jacket Designer: Nigel Partridge
Production Controller: Claire Rae

1 3 5 7 9 10 8 6 4 2

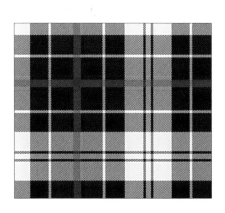

CONTENTS

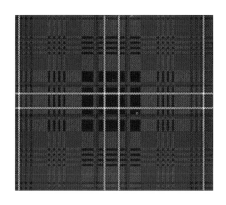

INTRODUCTION

All over the world, tartan is immediately recognized as a symbol of the Scottish people and their culture. It is glamorous, colourful and conjures up a romantic set of associations – the sway of the kilt, the skirl of the pipes, and brave Highlanders fighting for their rights.

The history of tartan lives up to these expectations. Over the centuries, its fortunes have ebbed and flowed. It has been mocked as the attire of savages, who were too poor to afford trousers; it has been outlawed, as the uniform of dangerous rebels; but ultimately it has triumphed, becoming a badge of honour not only for native Scots, but for their descendants around the globe.

CELTIC ROOTS AND HIGHLAND CULTURE

From ancient times the Celts, early inhabitants of the Highlands, enjoyed a high reputation as weavers, and they did much to develop the clan system, which has become so closely associated with the wearing of tartan.

▼ *Scotland's most romantic hero, Bonnie Prince Charlie.*

▲ *Tartan is produced in large quantities and endless variety.*

Although Scotland had won its independence early on in the 14th century, it was still a divided land. The Lowlands were increasingly drawn into the orbit of English affairs, while the Highlands remained isolated. The language was Gaelic, different religious and political views were held and the economy was different and much poorer. In purely physical terms, both the climate and the terrain could be challenging, while transport links were virtually non-existent, deterring all but the most intrepid visitor.

This isolation helped to preserve Highland dress and tartan, but at the same time it heightened a sense of disaffection. While the Stuart kings were on the throne, these feelings were kept in check, but after James VII lost his crown, many clans felt alienated. Events such as the Massacre of Glencoe (1692) and the Act of Union (1707), through which Scotland lost both its Parliament and its independence, moved much of the Highlands to the brink of rebellion.

THE BAN ON TARTAN

Succeeding generations have romanticized the two Jacobite uprisings (1715 and 1745), in which the Highland chiefs sought to restore the Stuarts to the British throne. In reality, they were unmitigated disasters from the rebels' point of view; they hastened the demise of the clan system and almost brought about the destruction of tartan itself.

For the uncompromising British solution was to root out the entire cultural system that had spawned the rebels. Tartan and Highland dress were among the prime targets. The ban on wearing tartan remained in force for a generation, so before it had even evolved into a recognized system for identifying the clan of the wearer, tartan seemed to be threatened with extinction.

REVIVAL

Tartan was rescued from obscurity by its links with the army, however. In a bid to boost recruitment for the new Highland regiments, which were needed to protect the interests of the growing British empire, the English government exempted soldiers from the ban. At the same time, the Romantic movement cast Highlanders in a new light. Increasingly, they were no longer seen as a threat to national security, but as the colourful and exotic descendants of the mysterious ancient Celts.

This change of image was confirmed in 1822, when George IV paid a state visit to Edinburgh. The event was a glorious pageant, in which the Highland clans took centre stage. The success of this venture had instant impact, and many of the elements of Highland costume only date back as far as this influential period. The romantic image of the Highlands was perpetuated by Queen Victoria, who developed a deep love for the area. At the same time, historians and enthusiasts endeavoured to document what they could of Highland culture.

MODERN DEVELOPMENTS

A similar dichotomy was apparent during much of the 20th century. On the one hand, the old romantic image of the Highlands began to degenerate into tourist cliché. It seemed as if tartan was destined to become little more than a form of packaging, for use on tins of shortbread or other souvenirs of Scotland. Equally, though, the expansion of tartan into other areas gave new life to the tradition. The creation

▶ *The sword and shield of a traditional Scottish warrior.*

▲ *Iqbal Singh, owner of a Scottish castle and his own tartan.*

of modern tartans started to accelerate in the 1950s. New designs covered a much broader range of themes, including commemorative and corporate tartans. Many of a considerable number of foreign tartans reflected a growing interest in traditional activities, such as Scottish country dancing and Highland games. In the United States and Canada there has been mounting interest in the celebration of Tartan Day. In addition, tartan has attracted the attention of fashion designers, and wearing Highland attire remains in vogue at celebrity events. Alongside all this, tartan has lost none of its power as an emotive symbol, however, and it is still a regular feature of purely Scottish landmark events and state occasions.

Purists may have their doubts about a few of the innovations, but the truth is that tartan is part of a living and ever developing tradition and, as such, a certain amount of change is inevitable. Far from diluting its Scottish character, the international scope of new tartan designs helps to strengthen and promote Scottish culture around the world.

TARTAN ORIGINS

THE STORY OF SCOTLAND'S NATIONAL DRESS IS BOUND UP
WITH THE COLOURFUL HISTORY OF THE HIGHLANDS.
THE CELTIC INHERITANCE AND THE UNIQUE COMPOSITION
OF THE HIGHLAND CLANS INSPIRED A LOVE OF THE BRIGHT
TARTAN CLOTHING THAT EVERY FAMILY WORE WITH PRIDE.

THE ORIGINS OF TARTAN

Although the origins of tartan extend far back into Scotland's past, the meaning of the term has changed over the centuries. Initially it referred to the type of cloth that was worn by Highlanders, rather than to its pattern, or to any notions of kinship. The word probably stemmed from the French *tiretaine* or *tertaine*, which described a coarse blend of linen and wool that is also known as linsey-woolsey.

THEORIES AND MYTHS

The derivation from the French is not universally accepted, but historical sources do offer some clues about the original purpose of tartan. It is apparent from the *Senchus Mor* ("Great Tradition"), an important anthology of documents relating to the legal system

Previous pages: Clunie Water, Braemar.

▼ *Part of a series of Roman carvings found near the Antonine Wall offers clues to the ancient Celtic style of dress.*

of the ancient Celts, that stripes were used as an indication of rank. Thus, a king's apparel would feature seven stripes, a druid's six, and so on down to the lowliest peasant, who was entitled to a single stripe. The colour of the stripes was also significant, and it seems possible that this symbolic form of attire provided inspiration for the initial development of tartan.

Alongside these perfectly feasible theories, there have been more speculative offerings. One scholar argued that the word emerged as a corruption of "Tartar", referring to the warlike people of central Asia. Another authority linked it with an Assyrian general named Tartan, who is mentioned fleetingly in the Bible (II Kings XVIII, 17 and Isaiah XX, 1) as the conqueror of the city of Ashdod. In both cases, the supposed link appears to be based on little more than a perceived similarity between the exotic and colourful Highland garb and that of the inhabitants of those distant, eastern regions.

GAELIC TRADITION

Some authorities claim that the word tartan comes from the Gaelic *tuar* ("colour") and *tan* ("district"), arguing that this accords well with the theory that the design of individual tartans originally indicated a region, rather than a specific clan. The proposition is tempting, but largely unsupported by documentary evidence. Instead, the earliest references to tartan in Gaelic texts invariably made use of the word *breacan*, meaning "speckled".

CONTEMPORARY SOURCES

The earliest information we have about the Celts is from their enemies, the Romans. The latter acknowledged that the Celts were skilled at weaving and dyeing, and they often commented on their love of colourful clothing. A fragment of a stone carving, discovered near the Antonine Wall in southern Scotland, shows Celtic warriors (either Picts or Caledonians) wearing something akin to the *sagum*, a type of military cloak. Like the plaid, which developed later, this was fastened at the shoulder with a pin or brooch.

From Ireland, the Scoti, or Scots, brought a garment known as a *leine croich* – a saffron shirt or tunic, perhaps made of linen, that extended almost to the knee. This was probably the dress described in the *Saga of Magnus Barefoot* (1093), the earliest known reference to the Highlanders' clothing. The saga describes how the Norwegian king, Magnus III, led an expedition to the Western Isles to force the Scots king, Edgar, to acknowledge his claim to the Hebrides. The campaign proved so successful that Magnus and his followers decided to adopt the local style

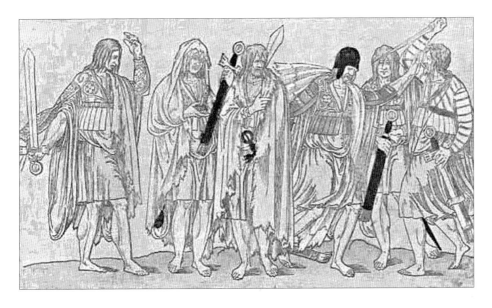

◀ *Early Highlanders wore variants of the* leine croich, *a linen tunic that originated in Ireland.*

of dress – "a short tunic and upper garments". Attempts have been made to interpret the tunic as an early version of the kilt; it is more likely that this was the *leine*, but the unclassified "upper garments" may well have been

▼ *Clansmen used a belt to gather up the long folds of their plaid and keep it in a manageable state.*

a precursor of the long woollen cloth known as a plaid. Either way, Magnus's new attire won him the nickname Barfod ("barefoot" or "barelegs").

This style of dress was slow to change, and more than four centuries later, the historian John Major described the garb of the Highlanders in similar terms. "From the middle of the thigh to the foot they have no covering for the leg, clothing themselves with a mantle instead of an upper garment, and a shirt dyed with saffron…"

THE POPULARITY OF PLAID
By the 16th century, there was growing evidence of the adoption of the plaid. In 1582, George Buchanan noted how some Highlanders were selecting the colours of their attire for camouflage rather than tribal allegiances: "They delight in variegated garments, especially stripes, and their favourite colours are purple and blue. Their ancestors wore plaids of many colours, and numbers still retain this custom, but the majority now in their dress prefer a dark brown, imitating nearly the leaves of the heather, that when lying upon the heath in the day, they may not be discovered…" Buchanan marvelled at their hardiness, facing the elements in their scanty apparel: "…in these [plaids], wrapped rather than covered, they brave the severest storms

in the open air and sometimes lay themselves down to sleep, even in the midst of snow…"

Tartan had already received the official seal of approval, for the 1538 accounts of the Lord High Treasurer reveal that James V was the first member of the royal family to order a Highland outfit. The items included "two and a quarter ells [1 ell = 1.1m/3¾ft] of variously coloured velvet for a short Highland coat at £6 per ell; three and a quarter ells of green taffeta, to line the said coat…and three ells of Highland tartan for the hose." In other words, the king was ordering a pair of tartan trews (tight trousers) and a short, multicoloured jacket.

▼ *John Speed's map of Scotland of 1646 showed Highlanders in skimpy plaids, emphasizing their poverty.*

WHAT IS A TARTAN?

In its structure, a tartan is essentially a checked pattern. This type of design is common to many cultures and can be traced back to prehistoric times. In Scotland, the earliest surviving example is the so-called Falkirk sett, which dates from the 3rd century AD. Excavated from a site near the Antonine Wall (a boundary wall erected by the Romans in southern Scotland), this tiny piece of fabric had been used as a stopper in an earthenware pot containing a hoard of silver coins. The cloth itself had not been dyed: its checked pattern was formed from the natural colouring of woven wool from brown and white varieties of Soay sheep.

This kind of simple woven checked pattern was used for centuries, in both the Lowlands and the Highlands, by shepherds for their plaids and *mauds*

▼ *On a loom, threads are stretched out lengthwise to create the warp, while those woven across it form the weft.*

or wraps, and came to be known as "the shepherd's plaid". The design is distinct from the clan tartans that developed at a later stage, since no symbolic overtones linked it to a particular place or group of people. Significantly, the tartan that it most resembles is the Scott Black and White, designed by Sir Walter Scott in 1822.

PATTERNS AND COLOURS

The pattern of an individual tartan is often described as a "sett". This refers to its structure, which was originally defined by exactly measuring the width of each stripe. More recently this method has been replaced by a precise thread-count. Some weavers are said to have kept a record of the early setts by colour-coding and numbering the threads on pattern-sticks.

Most setts are symmetrical. Each series of stripes is reversed around a

▲ *Found near Falkirk, this fragment of cloth is thought to be the oldest example of Scottish tartan.*

◀ *The shepherd's plaid, worn here by the poet James Hogg, is the simplest of all tartans.*

central stripe, known as the pivot. The blocks of pattern are then repeated in a regular fashion throughout the entire design. In a few cases, the structure of the sett is asymmetrical. Instead of reversing around pivots, these patterns are simply repeated over and over again. Additionally, in some of the older tartans, the sequences of stripes on the warp and the weft are different, and this also affects the symmetrical appearance of the design.

The colouring of individual setts may be described as "ancient" or "modern", which rather confusingly does not necessarily indicate the age of the sett. The term ancient refers to the colours produced by natural vegetable dyes, which were used until the mid-18th century and were generally very mellow in appearance. It may also be used to describe newer colours that imitate this natural effect. Modern colours are those produced using chemical dyes, which became available from the 1860s. As the precise shade of each colour was governed by the availability of dyes and the taste of individual weavers, different versions of the same tartan may look quite different and yet still be correct.

FUNCTIONALITY OF TARTAN

From an early stage, tartans were classified according to their purpose. In addition to their standard setts, many clans also adopted their own "dress" and "hunting" tartans. The latter were devised for those families who normally sported very bright colours, which were deemed unsuitable for the chase. In hunting setts, earthy colours such as muted browns and greens usually predominated. This did not mean that the outfit itself was necessarily plain. One of the earliest depictions of a hunting tartan was featured in John Michael Wright's portrait of Lord Mungo Murray. Painted in the early 1680s, the wearer's costume can only be described as ostentatious, even if the colouring is restrained.

TARTAN WEAVE

The checked pattern of a tartan is formed by interweaving two bands of stripes at right angles. First, the weaver sets the warp (the lengthwise threads) on the loom. The weft, or crosswise threads, are then woven into the warp. Traditionally, the patterns of the warp and the weft are identical, although it was not uncommon for slightly different yarns to be used to form each of these. For practical purposes, the yarn used for the warp is the stronger of the two.

The style of weave is known as twill. This means that each thread passes first over two and then under two of its crosswise counterparts. This produces the ribbed, diagonal effect on the length of material, where two different colours are blended. The only exception to this is the selvedge (the narrow border at the edge of the tartan), where a different style of weaving is often employed to prevent the fabric from unravelling.

By contrast, dress tartans were designed to be showy. They were used on formal occasions and have become popular wear at Highland dances. Generally, the design is a variant of the clan's normal tartan, but with one of the background colours changed to white. In direct contrast to the positive mood that dress tartans were meant to evoke, some clans also had special wear for periods of mourning. These are now rare, and the two Stewart mourning setts are among the very few that are still registered.

▲ *Wright's portrait of Mungo Murray shows how elaborate Highland dress could be when worn by the aristocracy.*

The *earasaid*, usually anglicized as "arisaid", provided another category of tartan. This garment, which was worn by many women in the Highlands and islands until the 18th century, was a large shawl or plaid that could also be used to cover the head. Some clans adopted specific tartans for arisaids. The MacLeod and Perry arisaids are among the few registered examples.

EARLY TARTAN CLOTHING

During the years when clan tartans were developing, Highlanders wore the designs in three ways: the belted plaid, the kilt, and trews. The respective merits of each were keenly debated from the outset, and the topic was to grow more contentious in later years.

By the 18th century, enthusiasts were producing pamphlets on the subject. Typical of this was the lively correspondence between the antiquarian John Pinkerton and Sir John Sinclair of Ulbster. In 1795, after hearing how the latter was championing the cause of trews, Pinkerton wrote to congratulate him: "When I first saw in the papers that you had appeared at court in a new Highland dress, substituting trousers or pantaloons for the

▼ *By fastening their plaid at the left shoulder, warriors were able to wield a weapon effectively with their right arm.*

THE KILT'S ORIGINS

There are numerous theories about the origins of the kilt. A controversial one is that it was invented by an Englishman, Thomas Rawlinson, who worked in the Glengarry iron works. Finding the plaid impractical, he divided it into two parts. The chief of Glengarry copied the idea and the kilt spread rapidly. Rawlinson's views on Highland attire are documented, but the notion that he invented the kilt remains questionable.

philabeg [kilt], I was highly pleased… The Highland dress is, in fact, quite modern and any improvement may be made without violating antiquity. Nay, the trousers are far more ancient than the philabeg."

THE VERSATILITY OF PLAID

The word "plaid" is sometimes used as a synonym for tartan, but it refers more specifically to the long woollen cloth worn over the shoulder. Supposedly first adopted by the Picts, such a cloth was formerly a standard form of dress among the ancient Scoti. The term has been linked to the Gaelic *plaide* ("blanket"), although this may have been a borrowing from a Scottish word already in use.

As a garment, the plaid was both simple and versatile. Essentially, it was a long, rectangular strip of fabric that required no sewing or tailoring. In order to put it on, the wearer first placed it on the ground, on top of his belt, and arranged it into pleats. He then lay down on it, fixing the belt around his waist and ensuring that the material reached down almost to his knees. When he stood up, the lower half of the plaid resembled a kilt. After donning a coat or jacket, the surplus material could either be looped over one shoulder, where it was attached with a brooch, or else employed as a cloak. Even after the advent of the kilt, the plaid remained a popular choice for Highlanders when they were engaged on military activities because, if they needed to sleep outdoors, it could also serve as a blanket.

THE HISTORY OF TREWS

Triubhas, or trews, also have a long history, and have sometimes been linked with the *braccae* (breeches) of the Gauls. They were close fitting and, in many cases, elaborately tailored. On the most expensive examples, the seams were decorated with gold braid or lace. Even on less costly items, the seams had to be carefully sewn so that the pattern matched. The checks of the tartans used to make trews were usually smaller than those used for plaids.

▲ Raeburn's portrait of Niel Gow (c.1796) shows a combination of breeches and hose of similar pattern.

There has been some debate about the occasions on which trews were worn. In his book *The Scottish Gael* (1831), James Logan suggested they were mainly intended for use by sick, lame or old Highlanders. Other sources have claimed that they were used in bad weather, or by Highlanders travelling in the Lowlands, who felt that they would look too conspicuous in a kilt. It has also been claimed that the garments carried class overtones, since they were frequently worn by chiefs and gentlemen, particularly when they were out riding.

As with the plaid, early illustrations show that trews took on many different forms. One popular variant was the use of matching breeches and stockings, which met at the knee. This combination is evident in Sir Henry Raeburn's portrait of Niel Gow, the celebrated fiddler. At first glance, he appears to be wearing a pair of tartan trews. Upon examination, however, it can be seen that he is wearing breeches buttoned along the side of the thigh. These reach down almost to his stockings, which are of a similar design.

WOMEN'S TARTAN

The plaid was also worn by women, usually in the form of a long shawl. On a visit to Scotland in 1636, Sir William Brereton noted that these garments were draped over their heads, covering their faces, "and would reach almost to the ground, but that they pluck them up, and wear them cast under their arms." A century later, the traveller Martin Martin observed that these plaids were predominantly white, with a few small coloured stripes, and that they were often fastened at the breast with a buckle. In the Highlands, the garment was usually known as an arisaid, or *tanac*. By the 18th century, tartan dresses had also become popular in some quarters. These were modelled on contemporary styles, with low-cut bodices and wide sleeves.

ARRIVAL OF THE KILT

The kilt was a comparatively late arrival in the tartan story, although there is considerable debate about the way it actually evolved. Initially, it was known as the *fèileadh beag* ("little plaid"), in order to distinguish it from the *fèileadh breacain* ("plaid of tartan") or the *fèileadh mor* ("big plaid"). It was commonly anglicized as "philabeg". The word "kilt" derives from Danish *kilte* ("to tuck up") and is related to the literal meaning of *fèileadh* ("folded").

▼ In the Highlands, the standard form of female attire was the arisaid. This example features the Sinclair tartan.

TRADITIONAL WEAVING

Travellers who toured the Highlands before the mid-18th-century ban on wearing tartan were much impressed by the standard of the weaving. Most were astonished that, in areas where many people lived on the poverty line, it was possible to produce clothing of such quality. In some communities there were professional weavers, but in the majority of cases everyday garments were produced at home by the women of the household.

By the end of the 1700s many commentators regretted the damage that had been done to Scotland's native weaving skills during the period of proscription. "The Act of 1746, discharging the Highland Dress, had the worst of consequences," lamented one citizen of Kincardine. "Prior to that period, the Highland women were remarked for their skill and success in spinning and dyeing wool, and clothing themselves and their households, each according to her fancy, in tartans, fine, beautiful and durable."

▼ *Weaving began on simple looms that were later modified for the Industrial Revolution.*

▲ *Female weavers often worked as a team, singing rhythmic "waulking" songs to ensure that they worked in unison.*

A HOME-BASED CRAFT

The preparation of the material was a lengthy process and involved a range of different skills – spinning and dyeing the wool, weaving, and fulling the lengths of cloth.

The wool had to be carded and spun into yarn before being dyed and woven. For the weaving, the women used small hand looms, throwing the shuttle from hand to hand, which placed limitations on the size of the items that could be produced. In many cases, it was necessary to sew two lengths of tartan together in order to create a standard plaid.

The most colourful process, however, was the fulling of the cloth, which was known as *luathadh*, or "waulking" the cloth. The purpose of this was to cleanse the wool of oil and shrink the cloth to thicken and felt it, making it

PATTERN-STICKS

According to the 17th-century observer Martin Martin, female weavers kept careful records of the patterns they used. In an account of his travels in the Western Isles, he noted that "the women are at great pains, first to give an exact pattern of the plad upon a piece of wood, having the number of every thred of the stripe on it."

Some authorities have cast doubt on the accuracy of this particular passage, however, since no original pattern-sticks have survived from the period prior to the ban on tartan.

▼ *Weavers were said to use pattern-sticks to help them remember the thread-counts of individual tartans.*

more hard-wearing. The cloth was washed in warm water and urine (used as a source of ammonia), then laid upon a board with a ribbed or uneven surface. A length of wattle-work was ideal for this but, if there was nothing else, a door would be taken off its hinges and placed on the ground. On the island of St Kilda, it was traditional to use a mat made of thick grass ropes. About a dozen women sat on either side of the cloth and kneaded it against the board. When their arms grew tired, they would waulk the material with their bare feet. They worked as a team, moving the cloth rhythmically and in unison. To help them co-ordinate their efforts, they would sing one of the many popular Highland waulking songs, which became louder and louder as the work progressed.

NATURAL DYES

The preparation of the dyes may have been equally picturesque, but details have long since been lost. Costume historians regret this, since the early Highland tartans were renowned for having colours that remained fast and did not fade. Many visitors reported having seen garments that were reputedly over a hundred years old but were still as brightly coloured as the day they came off the loom.

The dyes themselves mostly came from local vegetable sources. In the 19th century James Logan noted that although the Highlanders had little access to imported colours, "their native hills afforded articles with which they had found the art of dyeing brilliant, permanent and pleasing colours." He went on to say, "Every good farmer's wife was competent to dye blue, red, green, yellow, black, brown and their compounds. When we consider the care with which the Highlanders arranged and preserved the patterns of their different tartans, and the pride which they had in this manufacture, we must believe that the dyers spared no

pains to preserve and improve the excellence of their craft."

The most widely used dyes came from such items as bark, roots, moss, heather and bog-myrtle, but many Highlanders were evidently prepared to experiment. In the 1750s, Cuthbert Gordon of Banffshire produced a new purple dye, which he made out of a variety of lichens. He named this "cudbear" (after his first name) and marketed it with great success, after taking out advertisements in the *Scots' Magazine*. Similarly, when James Logan was researching for *The Scottish Gael*, he met a clansman who proudly declared: "Give me bullock's blood and lime, and I will produce you fine colours."

Perhaps the greatest accolade that these early dyeing techniques have received is the amount of time and effort that today's tartan manufacturers spend in trying to reproduce them. Synthetic dyes can appear harsh, and producers have taken great pains to mimic the "ancient" colours of the vegetable dyes. Significantly, the body that regulates the production of tartan has rejected suggestions that manufacturers should standardize their colours by adopting the international colour code.

▼ *Vegetable dyes could produce surprisingly bright, unfading colours.*

EARLY DISTRICT TARTANS

One of the main reasons why clansmen were able to develop their distinctive form of dress was the isolated nature of their homeland. Prior to the 18th century, travel in the Highlands was a difficult and dangerous affair. Transport links were virtually non-existent, some parts of the terrain were hard to cross, the climate could seem forbidding and, for southerners, the Gaelic-speaking areas presented language problems. None of these factors prevented a series of intrepid travellers from touring the northern regions, however, and the accounts they published have provided valuable information.

ASSOCIATIONS WITH LOCATION

Although accounts of this kind were often colourful and detailed, they shed very little light on the extent to which specific tartans were adopted by individual clans. Instead, the most telling account suggests that early tartans were a better indicator of place than of family. Martin Martin, who was himself a Gaelic-speaking Highlander, wrote the following in his *Description of the Western Isles of Scotland* (*c.*1695), one of the earliest books on the region: "The plad, worn only be the men, is made of fine wool, the thred as fine as can be made of that kind; it consists of

divers colours, so as to be agreable to the nicest fancy… Every Isle differs from each other in their fancy of making plads as to the stripes in breadth and colours. The humour is as different through the mainland of the Highlands, in so far that they who have seen those places are able, at the first view of a man's plad, to guess the place of his residence."

Martin's views have come under very close scrutiny, with experts seeking to iron out every possible ambiguity in his text. There has been discussion,

▲ *Since dyers used local materials, the colours of the landscape, as in this view of Ben Nevis and Inverlochy Castle, were echoed in many tartans.*

for example, of the precise meaning of "guess". Was this meant to convey any uncertainty on the author's part? Or was it simply an example of the narrower, 17th-century meaning of the word, roughly equivalent to "know"? Some commentators have argued that Martin's views are not incompatible with the idea that tartan grew out of

▼ *The Glen Orchy district tartan dates back to at least the early 1800s.*

▼ *The 18th-century Huntly district tartan may have Jacobite overtones.*

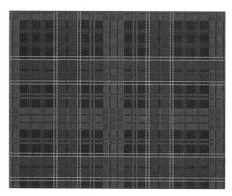

▼ *The Lennox is unusual in being both a district and a family tartan.*

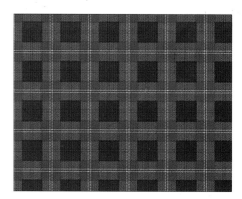

the clan system. Instead, they point out, his book underlines the close links that the clans had already forged with their ancestral territories.

LOCAL CLAN TARTANS

In spite of these reservations, the importance of the early district tartans is now readily acknowledged. In particular, historians have noted how some territorial setts – notably those of Old Lochaber, Lennox, Huntly and Glen Orchy – appear to have formed the basis of a number of local clan tartans.

The Huntly region, in north-east Scotland, provided one of the oldest known district tartans. Several clans were wearing it in the years leading up to the 1745 Jacobite uprising, among them the Gordons, the Forbes, the Munros, the MacRaes, the Rosses and the Brodies. Bonnie Prince Charlie is believed to have worn a variation of it while staying with the MacRaes, and his hosts appear to have employed it earlier in the century, when they fought at the battle of Sheriffmuir in 1715.

The prominent reds and greens of Huntly are reminiscent of several of the clan setts that were later introduced in this region, particularly those of the

▼ *The Falls of Arkaig are in the region of Lochaber, which produced one of the earliest known tartans.*

▲ *The Bridge of Orchy spans the River Dochard in the area that spawned the Glen Orchy sett.*

Munro, Ross and MacRae tartans. By contrast, the colour schemes that evolved in the Old Lochaber district, in the west Central Highlands, were far more muted and earthy. Lochaber lay in the heartlands of the Campbells and its tartan, which dates back to at least the 18th century, undoubtedly influenced their four main setts. It also has an affinity with the designs approved by the nearby MacDonald clan and with the principal military tartan, the Black Watch. The closest match, however, is with the Fergusson sett.

Situated in a picturesque stretch of Argyllshire, Glen Orchy is also in Campbell country. Its early district tartan appears to be one of the designs discovered by the agents of Wilson's of Bannockburn, the renowned tartan

manufacturers. Its structure, which features boxes within boxes with alternating light and dark squares, is reminiscent of several clan tartans of the area. These include the setts of the Stewarts of Appin, the MacGillivrays, the MacDonells of Keppoch, the MacIntyres and the MacColls.

The Lennox sett is actually a Lowland tartan, relating to a district north of Glasgow. Said to have been based on a lost 16th-century portrait, it can claim to considerable antiquity, and was certainly used as a source for some of the patterns introduced after the tartan revival of the 19th century.

HIGHLAND DRESS

Typical of 17th-century accounts of Highland clothing is the following extract from the writings of John Taylor, better known as the Water Poet. It describes the spectacle in 1618, when, at the invitation of the Earl of Mar, he joined a hunting party at Braemar.

"Their habit is shooes with but one sole apiece; stockings (which they call short hose) made of a warme stuff of divers colours, which they call tartane.

As for breeches, many of them, nor their forefathers, never wore any, but a jerkin of the same stuffe as their hose...with a plaed about their shoulders, which is a mantle of divers colours, much finer and lighter stuffe than their hose."

Taylor went on to stress that this form of dress was adopted by men of all classes, and was worn with a sense of pride.

THE CELTIC CONTEXT

The earliest tartans may have been notable for their geographical associations, but ultimately the links with the Highland clans were to prove far more significant. This extended family system traces its roots back to the nation's Celtic origins. The Celts spread their influence far and wide throughout Europe, and some elements of their social practices can be found elsewhere, particularly in Ireland, but it was the exceptional conditions in Scotland that enabled the clans to flourish.

CELTIC ANCESTRY

Initially an ancient people who flourished in central Europe, the Celts were mentioned in historical documents from the 6th century BC, but archaeologists have found hints that their culture may date back even further. In their heyday they were extremely powerful, even managing to sack the strongholds of Rome in 386 BC and Delphi in 279 BC. With the growth of the Roman Empire, however, their

▲ *This carving of Pictish warriors at Aberlemno may represent their victory over the Angles at Nechtansmere (685).*

influence declined and they were gradually pushed westwards, towards the fringes of the continent. Eventually, they were restricted to just a few areas beyond the confines of the empire. These included Scotland, Ireland, Wales, Cornwall and the region of Brittany in north-west France.

THE SCOTI

Rather than a single race, the Celts were a loose association of tribes. The Scoti, or Scots, were one such tribe, first

▼ *Located in the heart of Dalriada, this stone footprint was used during the inauguration ceremonies of chieftains.*

▲ *The name of the Caledonia tartan ultimately derives from a Celtic tribe based in the Tay valley area.*

recorded in the north-east of Ireland, where their principal sphere of influence was the tiny kingdom of Dál Riata, or Dalriada. Fierce intertribal conflicts prompted a group of Scoti to make the 19km/12-mile sea journey to the Argyll coast on the west side of Scotland, where they established a new settlement based on the rocky stronghold of Dunadd. This branch of Dalriada was founded in about AD 500. The kingdom remained divided for more than a century, but the Irish and Argyllshire Scoti maintained very close links. The latter gradually extended their influence in western Scotland, however, and severed ties with their homeland in Ireland.

THE PICTS

The Scoti were by no means the only Celtic tribe inhabiting the northern part of Britain. Their most illustrious rivals were the Picts.

Traditionally, these people were associated with the north-eastern areas of present-day Scotland, which was often described as Pictland. In common with the Scoti, however, they actually settled in a number of different regions in both Britain and Ireland. The Picts left no written records and, as a result, much of the information about their shadowy history is available only from Roman sources. Their name comes

from the Latin word for "the painted ones", alluding to their custom of painting or tattooing their bodies.

Very few Scottish families have managed to establish any link with this ancient people. Among the clans that claim Pictish descent are the Ogilvies, the Brodies, the Hendersons of Glencoe and the MacNaughtons. The latter have one of the stronger claims, given that their name derives from Nechtan, a celebrated Pictish king.

The Romans identified different tribes within the Picts. The most notable of these were the Venturiones, who were based in the tiny kingdom of Fortriu, which stretched from the Forth to the Tay, and the Caledonii, from whose name the Latin name for Scotland – Caledonia – is derived. In later years, it lost its precise historical meaning and came to be used as a poetic term for Scotland in its entirety. This trend peaked during the Romantic era, and the name's popularity at that time can be gauged by the fact that Caledonia was one of the very first fancy tartans produced by Wilson's of Bannockburn in 1819.

KENNETH MACALPIN'S ALBA

While the southern Celtic tribes wrestled for control with the Angles (the Germanic people who would eventually give their name to England) the Highlands were contested by the Scoti of Dalriada and the Picts. Their rivalry was eventually resolved in the mid-9th century by Kenneth MacAlpin, a Scot who gained the kingship of Dalriada in 840 but achieved real power only when he also acquired the Pictish throne seven years later.

This was not the first time that a single ruler had held both titles, but Kenneth managed to make the situation permanent. His own supporters claimed that his success was due to his mixed origins (his mother was a Pictish princess), though others believed it owed more to his brutal methods. The

rumours that he had murdered his Pictish rivals for the throne at a banquet persisted for generations.

Kenneth's enlarged kingdom was called Alba, or Albany, although by the end of the 9th century it was already better known as Scotland. Even though the territory did not include much of the Lowlands, the uniting of the two crowns is traditionally viewed as the first significant step in the creation of the Scottish nation. In the context of the clan system, this is reflected in the determination of many families to trace their lineage right back to MacAlpin himself. Alongside the more conventional dynasties, a group of clans define themselves as the Siol Alpin ("race of Alpin"), even though the true extent of their links with the ancient king is open to question. These clans include the MacNabs, the Grants, the MacKinnons and the MacAulays.

▼ *A medieval depiction of Kenneth MacAlpin, who managed to form a lasting union between Scots and Picts.*

SCOTTISH SURNAMES

Although most books about Highland clans and their tartans are structured around surnames, these were actually a comparatively late development. For centuries, most Europeans made use of patronymics, emphasizing the name of the individual's father: for example, Gregor, son of Donald. In Scotland, "son of" was conveyed by the Gaelic prefix *mac*, so he would be known as Gregor MacDonald. While this may have resembled a surname, it did of course change with each generation. Thus, Gregor MacDonald's son would be a MacGregor. This system proved confusing in written records and, in addition, made it hard to identify a person's clan from their name.

FIXED SURNAMES

In western Europe, the custom of using fixed surnames dates from around the 11th century. It developed initially in France, reaching some southern areas of Scotland in the following century. The Highlands were far more resistant to the idea, and the system did not really catch on until the 17th century.

Patronymics continued to be a common feature of fixed surnames. Increasingly though, the father in question was less likely to be the immediate parent. Instead, the patronymic usually referred to a distinguished ancestor, and within the context of a clan it was frequently applied to the dynasty's founder. In most cases, this ancestor was a genuine historical figure, but some surnames contained an aspirational element, as the genealogists of the clan strove to trace their descent from a legendary hero or ancient king, whose true lineage had long been lost.

The spelling of some names highlighted the differences between the Highlands and the Lowlands. The *mac* form, for example, was used in the former, while further south it was often anglicized as the suffix "son", as in Donaldson rather than MacDonald. The same meaning was also sometimes conveyed by adding "s" at the end of the forename; thus Andrews means "son of Andrew".

TERRITORIAL NAMES

While patronymics were the most ancient form of Scottish name, they were soon overtaken in popularity by territorial names. Most of these were based on the lands where the person lived, and this was certainly the system most favoured by the authorities. At the Council of Forfar in 1061, Malcolm III (r.1058–93) urged his subjects to adopt the practice. For a feudal ruler, the advantages were obvious, since it tied people to the land. However, territorial names were equally popular with clan chiefs, because they helped to bind their supporters to their ancestral homelands. Private landowners can often be identified through the uniquely Scottish phrase "of that Ilk". This means "of the same place", referring to the estate of the lord, or laird. A typical example of this form is the name of Sir Iain Moncreiffe, 24th of that Ilk, the genealogist and one of the foremost authorities on Scottish clans and tartans.

In many cases, territorial names indicated the origins of a person, rather than their place of residence. In Scotland, a high proportion of these were linked with locations in Normandy (such as Bruce, Cumming and Menzies). These ultimately stemmed from the aftermath of the Norman Conquest in 1066 for,

◄ *Many surnames reflect common medieval trades and pastimes. Hunting was an obvious source of names.*

although William I's followers settled in England, some of their descendants later began to migrate north in search of new opportunities.

In the same way, a few surnames offer clues to the nationality of a person. For obvious reasons, these names were applied to foreigners so that, although Scott is a common name in Scotland, it was more widely used south of the border. Instead, the most widely used national names were Inglis ("English"), Wallace (from a word that meant "foreigner", but was also linked to the root of Welsh) and Fleming ("Flemish"). As with the Norman names, these examples can sometimes be linked to specific historical events. It is no surprise, for instance, that the number of Flemings in Scotland increased after 1155, when Henry II expelled them from England.

OCCUPATIONAL NAMES

After territorial themes, the most common sources of Scottish surnames were occupations or trades. These were of particular relevance to the clans, since many of their ancestral leaders had acquired important hereditary posts. The most celebrated examples of this were the Stewarts, who derived their name from their role as high stewards

▼ *Scottish surnames often have religious links, as the Church was an extremely popular choice of profession.*

to the royal household. On a less exalted level, many names can be related to hunting (Hunter, Warren, Fletcher) or to trades related to clothing (Taylor, Glover, Dyer, Weaver) or cooking (Cook, Baker, Baxter). On a few occasions, records may even link some individuals with a specific job. Thus, one branch of the Porter family was so called after five generations had served as head gatekeeper at the abbey in Cupar Angus.

Many surnames have religious overtones. Here, the Scottish approach was markedly different from that in other Christian countries. For while, in most areas, children were simply given the name of a favourite saint, in Scotland

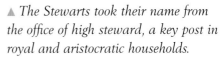

▲ *The Stewarts took their name from the office of high steward, a key post in royal and aristocratic households.*

this was often prefaced by a word that indicated they were a devotee of the holy man in question. The two most common forms were *maol* and *gille*, both of which denoted a servant. Thus the names Malcolm and MacCallum both indicated that the founder of the family was a follower of St Columba, while Gilchrist means "servant of Christ". Names of this kind usually indicated that the ancestor of the family had been a monk or a cleric. A few surnames specified this directly. Typical examples include MacNab ("son of the abbot"), MacTaggart ("son of the priest") and MacMillan ("son of the tonsured one").

NICKNAMES

Some Scottish surnames are based on nicknames. Often, these were colours that were used to describe the hair or complexion of the individual, while others were related to physical attributes. In addition, a number of surnames have Scandinavian origins, underlining the longstanding influence of the Vikings in northern and western Scotland.

THE CLAN SYSTEM

Due to their lack of political organization, throughout their long history the Celts failed to achieve any lasting territorial control. They compensated for this by developing tightly knit, extended family units that gave them cohesion at grass roots level and formed the basis of the clan system.

The Celts operated on a tribal basis, holding their land in common and owing their principal allegiance to a chief. Their basic territorial measurement was the *tuath*, or tribe, which was large enough to provide a fighting force of anything between 500 and 3000 men. Their simplest family grouping was the *derbfhine*, which spanned four generations, linking the descendants of a common great-grandfather. The word *clann* was used to describe a child or children, rather than having the broader sense of kinship that it came to acquire in Scotland.

THE CHIEF'S ROLE

At the heart of the system was the role of the chief. He offered protection to his clansmen, settled their disputes and led them in battle. In return, the clan members yielded to his authority on all

matters, granting him their unflinching loyalty. They also provided military service for him, as and when it was required. For their part, the chief's followers shared in a right of heritage known as *duthus*, which allowed them to settle and hunt on the clan lands held by their leader.

For these privileges, clan members paid a rent, which was collected and administered by the chief's "tacksmen", minor gentry who effectively acted as estate managers for their chiefs. Clansmen also benefited from a genuine feeling of equality. For, while the chief and his immediate entourage were held in high esteem, the main body of the clan was essentially classless. As the descendant of a distinguished ancestor, each member of the family could consider that they possessed a strain of gentility. "Though I am poor, I am noble," ran the motto of the MacLeans, while "As noble as a

◄ *Though borders fluctuated, this map provides a rough guide to the spheres of influence of the major powers.*

▲ *A Victorian painting of Rob Roy paying his rent due to the chief, to his representative, or tacksman.*

Scot" was a popular saying. Not surprisingly, perhaps, Scotland's southern neighbours were apt to poke fun at these attitudes. In the 18th century, in particular, English caricaturists frequently satirized the Scots for their obsession with their ancestry.

KEEPERS OF TRADITION

The clan's traditions were upheld by the "sennachie", one of the most important members of the chief's household. Learned in the clan's history, he maintained its records and genealogy, organized the inauguration of each new chief and addressed the host at clan gatherings. At times, the overriding emphasis on tradition could present problems. On more than one occasion, for example, an alliance between different clans was undermined by arguments over a family's customary right to occupy the most prestigious position in the battle formation.

The Picts

Dunkeld
Scone
Iona Dalriada Fortriu
Dunadd
ANTONINE WALL
Edinburgh
Strathclyde
The Angles
The Britons
HADRIAN'S WALL
Dalriada

Ulster

FOSTERAGE AND ALLEGIANCE

Within the clan, family ties were strengthened by an elaborate system of fosterage. Children were often brought up in the household of the chief or a relative. These youngsters were not necessarily orphans; instead, the practice was designed to bind the individual *derbfhine*, or family units, closer together. Fosterage was often a more important link than marriage. The Celts recognized several different types of union – some permanent, others distinctly not. In Scotland, a form of trial marriage, known as "handfasting", was particularly popular, until it was outlawed during the Reformation.

On an economic level, social ties were cemented by the system of "manrent". This was a bond contracted between individual clansmen and their chief. It involved the payment of "calps", or death duties, as a mark of allegiance to the leader, and in return for his

▼ *Kinship was all-important in Scotland so paintings of baptisms, like this one by John Phillip, were common.*

protection. This was payable even if the person in question was not actually living on the clan's estates. Although the practice was outlawed in 1617, it continued on an unofficial basis for many years.

RULES OF SUCCESSION

The various Celtic societies also had a distinctive attitude to the question of succession. They did not insist on primogeniture (the automatic right of inheritance by the firstborn, male child), even if in practice this was often what happened. In many cases, the succession would instead be granted to the most able or the most suitable member of the family units. The heir was nominated during the life of the chief, and was known as the tanist ("second"). There was some variation within the different Celtic communities. The Picts, for example, were unusual in favouring matrilinear succession (that is, through the female line).

The strength of the Highland clan system can be gauged by the fact that it survived the advent of feudalism. On

the face of it, these two organizational structures might seem to be totally incompatible. The clans were essentially tribal in nature, while feudalism was strictly hierarchical, with all power and possessions deriving ultimately from the king. Alone among the Celtic nations, Scotland found a compromise between the two opposing forces. In its hierarchy, the king was recognized as a type of supreme chief, comparable with the high kings of ancient Ireland.

In effect, the early Scottish rulers had little choice but to accept this compromise, given that large parts of the country remained outside direct royal control until the later Middle Ages. This was particularly true in the western isles and the north, where the Scandinavian influence was very strong. Once the nation was genuinely unified, the dual loyalties of the clansmen – to their chief and to the king – became a potential problem. When these conflicted, as they did during the time of the Jacobite rebellions, the authority and independence of the clan chiefs became all too apparent.

COMPOSITION OF THE CLANS

Many clans are described as "septs", but since the term covers a variety of different situations this is a highly contentious issue. In its loosest sense, it can suggest followers or dependants, and usually refers to those families who attached themselves to larger clans for reasons of protection, or else to branches within a clan that boasted a surname that was different from their kinfolk (for example the MacIans of clan Donald). However, it can also allude to the complications that arose when patronymic surnames were fixed. The person in question might "freeze" his name to include his father, or else he might choose to honour a more distant ancestor. Either way, this might make it difficult to assess which was his rightful clan.

ADOPTED NAMES

Alongside their "native men" (blood relations), many clans contained "broken men". These were Highlanders who, for one reason or another, could no longer use their own names. The most celebrated example of this was the MacGregor clan. After accusations

of violent conduct, the name of MacGregor was outlawed in 1603, forcing the clansmen to take other names. Failure to comply with this order amounted to a crime that was punishable by death. For more than a century, the MacGregors were persecuted in this way, living, in Sir Walter Scott's words, as "children of the mist" until the ordinance was repealed in 1774. The most famous of these shadowy figures was Rob Roy, whose career as an outlaw was romantically retold in one of the author's novels.

In order to enhance the power and prestige of their followers, clan chiefs did their utmost to swell clan numbers. Often, they would try to persuade families who were living on their land to adopt their surname. Indeed, some cases were also reported of payments being made to poorer tenants if they would agree to rename their children. In most instances, the families in question needed very little prompting. In an

◀ *One of Waitt's portraits of the Laird of Grant's retinue shows Alastair Grant Mor, the chief's champion.*

▲ *Cattle stealing was endemic in the Highlands; the authorities tried to curb it by outlawing the worst offenders.*

age when surnames were still very fluid, it was common for people to take their name from the place where they lived. Scott himself gained first-hand experience of the consequences of moving from one clan territory to the next, when he was travelling through the Highlands. His guide called himself a Gordon, but the writer was convinced that on a previous meeting he had known him by another name. "Yes, certainly," the fellow confirmed, "but that was when I was living on the other side of the hill."

CLAN TARTAN AS LIVERY

Like the clan name, tartan was not used exclusively as the badge of an individual's family or clan; it could also be employed as a form of livery. Throughout the Middle Ages, many chiefs maintained princely courts in the old Celtic fashion. Their retainers included poets and musicians, who held their posts on a hereditary basis

▲ *Music was important in Celtic courts; most chiefs employed a harpist and piper, both hereditary posts.*

and were often dressed in the livery of their masters, irrespective of their own family origins.

The practice of using a clan tartan as livery for retainers survived well into the 18th century, as is confirmed by a remarkable series of portraits belonging to the Grants. This mighty clan reached the peak of its influence in the late 17th century. Ludovic Grant, the 8th Lord of Freuchie, was so powerful that he earned the nickname of the Highland King. In 1694, William II (William III of England, r.1689–1702) rewarded him for his support by granting him the Regality of Freuchie, a rare honour that enabled him to rule like a monarch on his own lands.

In 1710, Ludovic resigned the regality, transferring power to his son Alexander. This took place at a ceremonial gathering of the clan, at Balintome in Strathspey. According to William Fraser, writing in the 19th century, on this grand occasion, "all the gentlemen and commons of his name" were commanded to appear, "wearing whiskers and making all their plaids and tartan of red and green". Determined to maintain the exalted reputation of his clan, Alexander decided to create a new portrait gallery at Castle Grant, containing pictures of

his immediate family as well as the leading members of his household. The artist Richard Waitt (d.1732) embarked upon the project in 1713.

Although some of the portraits are now dispersed, the Grant collection is notable for two reasons. First, it underlines how loosely the notion of a clan tartan was applied. Officially, the Grants were expected to wear a sett of dark green and red, but a precise design was not specified. This somewhat vague stipulation was enforced only during periods of conflict. In peacetime, clansmen were allowed to wear the plaid of their choice. As a result, no two figures in the Grant portraits are wearing identical tartans. More significantly still, the collection includes paintings of members of the chief's retinue, dressed in livery. The most impressive of these is the picture of William Cumming, piper to the lord of Grant. Behind him is displayed the lord's standard, showing his arms and motto, together with a view of Castle Grant.

▼ *Richard Waitt's portrait of the piper William Cumming is unusually elaborate in its detail.*

FOREIGN INFLUENCES

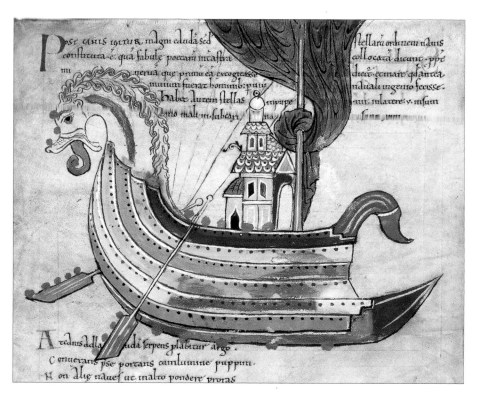

Both tartans and the clan system had their roots in the customs of the ancient Celts, but these traditions did not survive in their purest forms. The early years of the Scottish nation were precarious in the extreme, as invaders threatened on every side.

VIKING RAIDERS

Even as Kenneth MacAlpin united the Picts and the Scots, the borders of his new kingdom were assailed by Viking raiders. The first record of attack on the boundaries of present-day Scotland dates from 794, when Vikings plundered some of the remote northern isles. Their raids increased in both frequency and ferocity through the 9th century. In 849, just two years after coming to the throne, Kenneth felt compelled to remove some of the relics of St Columba, Scotland's most important saint, from the island of Iona to a safer location in the east.

In the north, the Vikings eventually established the earldom of Orkney, which at times encompassed large

▲ A Viking longship, pictured here in an 11th-century manuscript, would have struck fear into Scottish hearts.

tracts of Caithness and Sutherland. In the west, they occupied the Hebrides, becoming Lords of the Isles. This dominance persisted for several centuries, and only with defeat at the battle of Largs in 1263 did the Vikings' influence begin to wane.

As a result, several of the major clans have Viking origins. The founder of the MacLeods, for example, is traditionally thought to have been a Viking prince called Leod, the younger son of King Olaf the Black, who ruled over Man and the North Isles. Olaf himself came from the distinguished royal line of Godred Crovan, who had ruled over Dublin and the Hebrides.

In the same way, the MacDonalds are said to stem from Reginald, the son of Somerled, most famous of the self-styled kings of the Isles. Subsequent MacDonald chiefs continued to style themselves by this title, ruling their

domains independently, until the Stewarts suppressed the Lordship of the Isles in 1494.

This Scandinavian influence did much to strengthen the development of the clans. Somerled, for instance, was an enthusiastic supporter of the Celtic traditions in his homeland, far preferring them to the process of anglicization that was being carried out by the Scottish kings. He even tried to revive the Celtic church, by creating a new foundation on Iona.

ANGLO-NORMAN REFORMS

In this respect Somerled was swimming against the tide. Celtic rule in Scotland had effectively come to an end with the reign of Macbeth (r.1040–57). Public perceptions of this monarch

▼ The actor William Macready presents the popular image of Macbeth in a scene from Shakespeare's play.

▲ *Malcolm Canmore's pious wife Margaret (c.1046–93) is idealized in stained glass in Edinburgh Castle.*

have been given a very negative slant through Shakespeare's play, but in fact he was neither a murderer nor a tyrant. By the standards of the time he was a peaceable and popular ruler, who travelled to Rome as a pilgrim and donated money to the poor. On his death, Macbeth was accorded the ancient privilege of being buried with the old Celtic kings on Iona.

Macbeth was the last of the Scottish kings to rule from the Highlands. With the accession of Malcolm Canmore as Malcolm III in 1058, the country became increasingly prey to influences

▶ *David I (left) is enthroned beside his grandson and successor, Malcolm IV, in an elaborate example of Celtic calligraphy.*

from the south. Malcolm himself had been raised at the Saxon court of Edward the Confessor (r.1042–66), where he also learned much about Norman ways.

Crucially for the clans, Malcolm changed the law of succession, replacing the old Celtic system of tanistry with the primogeniture that was common in mainland Europe. English influences were pressed even further by Malcolm's wife, Margaret, who two centuries later, in 1249, was canonized as St Margaret. She introduced wideranging reforms to the church in Scotland, replacing the Celtic rites that had been championed by St Columba with practices advocated by the Papacy. As part of this reorganization she placed the Scottish church under the jurisdiction of the Archbishop of York.

THE NEW FEUDAL SYSTEM

With the coming of the Normans, Scotland was drawn still further into the European orbit of affairs. This gathered pace during the reign of David I (r.1124–53). More than any Scottish king before him, he had divided loyalties. He was the brother-in-law of the English king, Henry I (r.1100–35), and

had grown up at his court. Prior to his accession to the Scottish throne, he had also established himself as one of the most powerful barons south of the border. A judicious marriage brought him the earldom of Northampton and Huntingdon, and he also owned extensive lands in Northumberland.

Given this background, it is hardly surprising that David reshaped his new kingdom in the image of the Anglo-Norman world he had known since his youth. Feudalism was introduced, along with a new system of justice and a string of castles designed to bolster royal authority. The feudal structure cut across the old notion of ancestral clan estates. Instead, all land was owned by the king, who granted it through charters in return for loyal service. Often, the two systems co-existed quite happily, but the monarch's increased power offered scope for future conflict: by granting one chief a charter to land that had traditionally been held by a rival, it was possible for the king to weaken the clans by playing them off against each other.

Upon his accession, David made many grants of land in Scotland to his Norman followers. This provoked considerable discontent in the Highlands, where there was talk of an "invasion by invitation", and there were sporadic uprisings in some areas that were Gaelic-speaking. However, a substantial number of today's clansmen are descended from the Norman adventurers. The most significant newcomers were Robert de Brus and John de Bailleul, whose descendants – Robert the Bruce and John Balliol – were to play a crucial role in Scotland's struggle for independence.

THE WAR OF INDEPENDENCE

Scotland's increasing ties with England enabled it to develop an efficient government broadly in line with much of continental Europe, but raised concerns that the country might be swallowed up by its powerful southern neighbour.

A CRISIS OF SUCCESSION

The threat became a reality in 1286, when Alexander III suddenly died, causing a succession crisis that threw Scotland into turmoil. His heir was his infant granddaughter, the so-called Maid of Norway. The English king, Edward I (r.1272–1307), saw an opportunity and proposed that his son, Prince Edward, should marry the child. The implication – the union of England and Scotland – was very clear. However, the Maid died on the voyage from Norway to Britain, re-opening the succession debate. More than a dozen claimants to the throne came forward, the most realistic candidates being Robert Bruce

the Competitor (the grandfather of Robert the Bruce) and John Balliol. In a bid to prevent bloodshed, Edward was invited to preside over the court that decided between the two men. Robert claimed he had been nominated as tanist (heir apparent) by the previous monarch, Alexander II (r.1214–49), but Balliol, who had the stronger case under the law of primogeniture, won the decision and was duly made king in 1292.

The disadvantages of the feudal system now became all too apparent. Balliol owned land in England, which meant that he owed fealty to Edward as his overlord, and Edward exploited this loophole to rule Scotland in all but name. As a vassal, Balliol was commanded to render military service and help fund Edward's campaigns in France. The English king also encouraged disgruntled claimants in Scottish courts to appeal to the higher authority of the courts in the south.

▼ *Robert the Bruce is depicted as a courtly knight, with his second wife Elizabeth, daughter of the Earl of Ulster.*

▼ *John Balliol's act of subservience in paying homage to Edward I lost him the respect of most Scots.*

The document known as the Ragman's Roll, on account of the ragged tangle of ribbons that hang from its seals, records one of the darkest moments in Scotland's history, when its nobility had to swear allegiance to Edward I of England in 1296. Containing almost 2000 signatures – representing virtually all the leading figures of the day – it provides a snapshot of the country's political structure and offers an important insight into the development of the clans. Many genealogists have found this document an invaluable source of information for, although a chief may claim descent from some ancient worthy, the Ragman's Roll often presents the first concrete evidence of their ancestry.

BALLIOL'S REBELLION

Not surprisingly, these measures provoked Balliol into rebellion. He forged an alliance with the French king and prepared to march on England. Edward had expected no less and, in 1296, launched a devastating response. His army swept through the Lowlands, plundering Berwick before defeating Balliol at Dunbar. To consolidate his victory, he seized the Stone of Scone – the inaugural stone of the Scottish kings – and carried it off to England. He also compelled the leaders of the defeated nation to assemble at Berwick and sign a declaration that recognized him as king of Scotland.

The speed and ease of Edward's victory had highlighted a weakness of the clan system: a tendency to place personal squabbles before national unity. Nothing illustrates this more forcibly than the rivalry between Balliol and

Bruce. For, when the former was trying to forge an alliance against Edward I, the Bruces deliberately snubbed him. In retaliation, Balliol seized their estates in Annandale and granted them to his relative, Red John Comyn. Robert the Bruce (the grandson of Balliol's rival) exacted his revenge several years later, when he stabbed Comyn during a quarrel in a Dumfries churchyard. This incident was all the more tragic, given that the pair had arranged to meet precisely to organize a plan of action against their English enemy.

WILLIAM WALLACE AND ROBERT THE BRUCE

Edward had knowingly exploited this kind of feuding in order to gain control of Scotland. However, the events of 1296 provoked a response that caught him unawares. First, in 1297, an uprising led by Sir William Wallace produced an unexpected victory over the English army at Stirling Bridge. Edward responded with his customary ferocity, inflicting a crushing defeat on

▼ *The stabbing of John Comyn was a pivotal event, prompting Robert the Bruce to make a bid for the throne.*

the rebels at Falkirk the following year. Wallace managed to evade capture for a time, but was eventually caught and executed in 1305.

Edward may have thought that he had extinguished all sparks of resistance, but Wallace's revolt was swiftly followed by a new rebellion. After Robert the Bruce stabbed Red John Comyn he needed to take decisive action. The fact that the killing had taken place on holy ground made it a

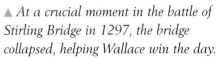

▲ *At a crucial moment in the battle of Stirling Bridge in 1297, the bridge collapsed, helping Wallace win the day.*

sacrilege, which laid Robert open to excommunication by the Church – a punishment that would snuff out any possible claim to the throne. So he marched straight to Scone and declared himself king of the Scots.

This daring act of defiance ultimately proved successful for two main reasons. First, Edward died suddenly of dysentery as he travelled north to lead a counterattack against the Scots. More importantly, Robert the Bruce's rebellion finally managed to unite the clans against a common enemy. The key victory took place at Bannockburn in 1314, when he mobilized a Celtic army composed of more than 20 clans. These included the Camerons, the Campbells, the Chisholms, the Frasers, the Gordons, the Grants, the Gunns, the Mackays, the Mackintoshes, the MacPhersons, the MacQuarries, the MacLeans, the MacDonalds, the MacFarlanes, the MacGregors, the Mackenzies, the Menzies, the Munros, the Robertsons, the Rosses, the Sinclairs and the Sutherlands. The reward for their unity was independence.

THE SUPPRESSION OF TARTAN

AS RIVALRY WITH ENGLAND TURNED TO OUTRIGHT REBELLION, TARTAN BECAME A SYMBOL OF SCOTS PATRIOTIC FERVOUR AND NATIONAL UNITY. RECOGNIZING THIS, THE GOVERNMENT DID ITS UTMOST TO SUPPRESS IT, BY BANNING THE WEARING OF HIGHLAND DRESS.

CAUSES OF DISSENT

The military successes of Robert the Bruce may have won independence for the Scots, but the close genealogical links between the royal families of England and Scotland ensured that the threat of new claimants from the south remained strong. This problem eventually resurfaced at the beginning of the 17th century.

Initial fears were mainly experienced by the English. For much of her reign, Elizabeth I (r.1558–1603) was concerned about the claim of her kinswoman Mary, Queen of Scots, to the English throne, and she eventually had her executed in 1587. In spite of this, after the death of Elizabeth Mary's son, James VI of Scotland, inherited the English throne as James I. This did not present an immediate cause for concern north of the border, where James had been king since 1567, as his outlook was undoubtedly Scottish. During his early years in London he was viewed with suspicion by the English. Significantly, when the idea of creating

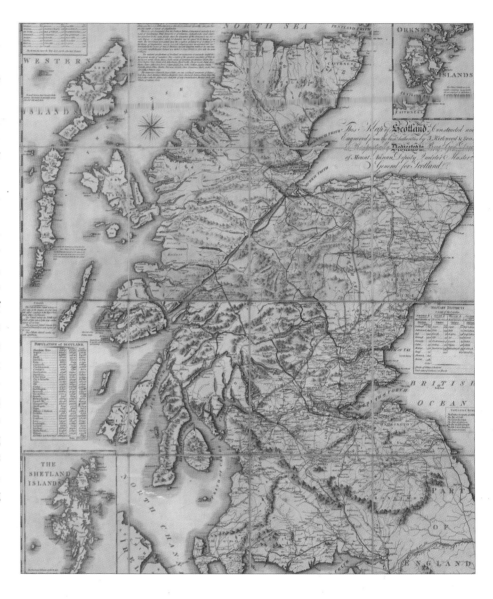

▲ *A 1804 map of Scotland, showing the Highland Line in green, running north-east from the Firth of Clyde.*

▼ *Mary, Queen of Scots, being led to execution in 1587, after long years of imprisonment by her cousin, Elizabeth.*

a permanent union of the two crowns was mooted in 1607, the English parliament dismissed the idea.

James's reign, however, did accentuate the growing gulf between the Highlands and the Lowlands. Although politically the two regions were both part of Scotland, their social, religious and linguistic differences were so deeply rooted that they remained separate countries in all but name. This

Previous pages: Ruthven Barracks.

concept of a divided land was widely accepted until early modern times. It was epitomized by the Highland Line, from Argyllshire in the west to Aberdeenshire in the east, which was set down as a boundary line for different rates of taxation in an Act of Parliament of 1784 dealing with whisky production.

With the accession of James VI to the English throne, the Lowlands were drawn increasingly into the orbit of English affairs, while the Highlands remained marginalized. The bonds between England and the Lowlands began to seem much stronger than the links between the two Scottish regions. To a large extent, this was deliberate government policy. James introduced a number of measures designed to "civilize" the Highlands by undermining the old Gaelic culture with its clan system. Many chiefs were ordered to prove their right to their long-held ancestral territories by presenting their charters, or else paying for new ones. The king was equally determined to cut the size and influence of their princely households, specifying in particular that the maintenance of bards "and other idlers" was forbidden, in a measure directed

▼ *After James VI's accession to the English throne in 1603, Scotland was increasingly ruled from the south.*

against the clan sennachies. In addition, members of the gentry were required to send their eldest sons to be educated in the Lowlands to ensure that they learned English.

THE FIFE ADVENTURERS

James also sought to weaken Celtic influence by introducing Lowland settlers into key areas of the country. The most infamous example of this policy took place in Ireland, where "plantations" of English and Lowland settlers were established at the expense of local families. Similar schemes were adopted in the Highlands, the most notorious instance occurring on the island of Lewis. In 1598, it was granted to a Lowland company known as the Fife Adventurers, headed by the Duke of Lennox, the king's cousin.

The Adventurers' charter authorized the company "to plant policy and civilization in the hitherto most barbarous Isle of Lewis...and to develop the extraordinarily rich resources of the same for the public good and the king's profit." In doing so, its representatives were given leave to carry out whatever "slaughter, mutilation, fyre-raising, or utheris inconvenities" were deemed necessary. Ultimately, this was to no avail, since there was stiff resistance from the inhabitants, mobilized by the dominant local clan, the MacLeods. The company's camps were looted and its livestock seized, and by 1610 it was bankrupt. But James had his revenge: the Adventurers sold their interests to the Mackenzies of Kintail, who ultimately supplanted the MacLeods.

THE RISE OF PRESBYTERIANISM

In the long term, religion was to prove an even greater source of discord. James was anxious to bring Scottish modes of worship into line with English practice, and he sought to put this policy into effect through the Five Articles of Perth in 1618. In the Lowlands, however, Calvinism (a strict

▲ *An influential Reformation figure, John Knox popularized the austere teachings of John Calvin in Scotland.*

form of Protestantism) had already taken root, largely through the efforts of John Knox (*c*.1513–72). This doctrine repudiated the hierarchical set-up of the Church, believing that it should be run by ministers (presbyters) of equal status, rather than bishops. As a result, Presbyterianism became the dominant religious force in Scotland. In general, these ideas were received less enthusiastically in the Highlands, where there was widespread support for more traditional forms of worship.

HIGHLAND UNITY

In spite of their growing isolation from the Lowlanders, the Highland clans remained as tightly knit as ever. One important example of this occurred in 1618, when Sir Robert Gordon of Gordonstoun wrote to Murray of Pulrossie, asking him "to remove the red and white lines from the plaids of his men, so as to bring their dress into harmony with that of the other septs". The original letter has not survived, and the surviving copy may be a forgery. If the message is genuine, however, it constitutes one of the earliest attempts to harmonize a tartan within a clan in order to promote a sense of unity.

THE END OF STUART RULE

By the reign of Charles I (r. 1625–49), the Scots had become closely identified with the Stuart cause. This led them to take part in the king's religious conflicts, as well as the Civil War (1642–49), which ultimately cost him his life. For many Highlanders, the consequences of supporting the Stuarts were severe. After the execution of Charles I, his son made a determined attempt to recapture the throne, which ended in failure at the battles of Dunbar in 1650 and Worcester in 1651. These defeats were followed by the transportation of many clansmen to the Americas. After Dunbar, for example, some 900 Scottish prisoners were sent as bond-servants to Virginia, and a further 150 to New England. Similarly, over the next few years, around 270 men were deported to Boston, while others were taken to the new colony of Jamaica.

Following the restoration of the monarchy in 1660, the Scots maintained reasonable relations with the Stuart kings. Charles II (r. 1660–85) was well disposed towards the country where he had first been crowned king (at Scone in 1651), although his rule there was marred by continuing religious divisions. The brief reign of Charles's brother, James VII (James II of England, r. 1685–88), was more troubled. Prior to his accession, he had served successfully as viceroy in Scotland, working with the clan chiefs to pacify the Highlands. However, he never returned north after ascending the throne and, ominously perhaps, he was the first ruler of his country not to take the Scottish coronation oath or to be crowned in Scotland.

THE JACOBITE CAUSE

James was a Catholic, and his determination to remain true to his faith lost him support in both England and

▲ *This Dutch engraving shows the execution of Charles I, outside the Banqueting House, Whitehall, in 1649.*

▼ *A highland warrior, complete with tartan trews, bonnet and plaid, a mode of dress that astonished the English.*

Scotland. It was the birth of his son James, a Catholic heir, that finally galvanized his opponents into chasing him from the throne. In the aftermath, the Protestant William, Prince of Orange, the Dutch Stadtholder, and his wife Mary, James's daughter, were invited to rule jointly in his place.

This marked a decisive shift in Scottish politics. For, while the Scottish Convention of Estates followed their English counterparts and voted to offer the throne to William and Mary, the decision was by no means unanimous. There were many who felt that, even if James VII was deemed to have abdicated, his infant son James was the rightful heir to the Scottish throne.

They described themselves as Jacobites, taking their name from Jacobus, the Latin form of James. For the following 70 years, this faction presented a genuine threat to the authority of the government in London.

The first insurrection against the new order manifested itself at the battle of Killiecrankie in 1689, when the Jacobite clans massed against William's troops. The Highland army was raised in the traditional manner of the clans, with a fiery cross carried through the glens. The Scottish forces won the day, but their charismatic leader, John Graham, Viscount Dundee (better known as Bonnie Dundee), was killed, and without him the rebels were soon dispersed. During these campaigns, Highland warriors made some rare excursions outside their native region, when their "antique" style of dress astonished Lowlanders and Englishmen alike. The novelist and pamphleteer Daniel Defoe, for example, noted, "Their swords were extravagantly, and I think insignificantly long... These fellows looked when drawn out like a regiment of Merry-Andrews [buffoons] ready for Bartholomew Fair."

THE GLENCOE MASSACRE

Although the uprising was obviously a cause for concern, the majority of Scots were still open-minded about the new administration. This soon changed, however, following one of the most shameful episodes in Scottish history. In a bid to make peace, William offered the hostile Highland chiefs an olive branch by granting them an amnesty, provided that in return they swore a personal oath of allegiance to him.

The final date by which this oath had to be taken was 1 January 1692, but through a chapter of accidents, Alasdair MacIain, chief of the MacDonalds of Glencoe, missed the deadline by five days. William mistakenly interpreted this as an act of insubordination and decided to make

TARTANS OF THE *GRAMEID*

The first Jacobite uprising inspired the *Grameid*, an epic poem written in Latin, supposedly by a loyal standard-bearer. Modelled on Virgil's *Aeneid*, it features stirring descriptions of Highland dress. MacNeill of Barra sported a plaid that "rivalled the rainbow", while the multicoloured coat of Lochiel and the scarlet and purple outfits of Glengarry's men also gave rise to notable verses. For costume historians, the *Grameid* has proved something of a mixed blessing, since none of the patterns described bears any resemblance to existing tartans, and there are suspicions that they are colourful examples of poetic licence. Even if this is so, it is nonetheless significant that descriptions of tartan were being used as an expression of patriotic fervour.

an example of the MacDonald clan. Accordingly, the order went out "to fall upon the rebels...and put all to the sword." The instruments of the king's justice were the Campbells, who had been billeted with the MacDonalds for a fortnight. On the night of 13 February, they set upon their hosts while they lay in their beds, killing at least 38 men, and set fire to their homes. The casualties would have been higher, but for the fact that a violent snowstorm was raging and some of the intended victims escaped into the hills.

The Glencoe massacre proved to be a huge miscalculation on William's part: far from intimidating his Scottish subjects, it united them in outrage. The cowardly nature of the attack, the fact that many women and children died after being turned out into the snow, and the way that the Campbells had contravened the laws of hospitality combined to strengthen Jacobite sympathies throughout the country.

▼ *The Glencoe massacre, shown in this artist's impression, actually took place at night, in the middle of a snowstorm.*

THE ACT OF UNION

In the early years of the 18th century, a new menace began to cast a shadow over the Highland way of life. William II died in 1702 and was succeeded by Anne, the younger daughter of James VII. Though she had conceived 19 children, most of them were either stillborn or miscarried, and the only one to survive infancy had died in 1700, at the age of 11. It was clear that Anne's eventual death would be followed by a succession crisis.

Those with the strongest claim to the throne were the Stuarts. This delighted the Jacobites, of course, but appalled the English, since the Stuart family were still staunch Catholics. As a result, it was decided that the succession would eventually pass to George of Hanover, who was distantly related to James VI. This arrangement was acceptable to members of the English parliament, but it seemed unlikely that their Scottish counterparts would agree to it. The only

▼ *Women wore tartan to show their Jacobite sympathies, as in this portrait attributed to Cosmo Alexander.*

solution was to join the two countries on a permanent basis, uniting them under a single crown.

After much argument, the Act of Union was passed in 1707. Using a combination of bribery and blackmail, the English government eventually persuaded the Scottish parliament to vote itself out of existence in return for a number of economic benefits. Although the move was carried through quite legally, it attracted considerable opposition in Scotland. For many, it seemed that the nation's liberties had been sold off to its southern rival.

TARTAN AS A SYMBOL OF RESISTANCE

The Scottish public showed their discontent in a variety of ways and, for the first time, these included the use of tartan. Significantly, its use in this fashion was not limited to the Highlands. Even prosperous Edinburgh ladies registered their protest by wearing a tartan accessory or using it as a decorative material in their homes. Sir Walter Scott confirmed this many years later when he wrote: "I have been told, and believed until now, that the use of tartans was never general in Scotland until the Union, with the detestation of that measure, led it to be adopted as the National colour, and the ladies all affected tartan screens [scarves]…"

TARTAN IN PORTRAITS

The growing use of tartan in portraiture also dates from this period. Once again, the trend covered a broad spectrum of people. It was shortly after the Act of Union, for example, that the Grants decided to create a portrait gallery showing the family and their household attired in Highland dress. At the same time, an attempt was made to standardize the clan sett as a "tartane of red and green, set broad-spring'd".

▲ *In Waitt's portrait, Lord Duffus wears a belted plaid with loose folds of cloth gathered below the tunic.*

The Grants were firm government supporters and they went on to oppose the Jacobites in the 1715 rebellion. It is clear, therefore, that in the case of this clan the use of tartan held no political overtones. The same can also be said of the early 18th-century portrait of Sir Robert Dalrymple. Like the Grants, he had close connections with the Whig government of the day. Indeed, he was a relative of James Dalrymple, the royal Secretary of State in Scotland who had borne much of the blame for the Glencoe massacre. Robert Dalrymple's portrait is particularly interesting because it provides one of the earliest illustrations of a Lowlander wearing tartan. The sitter is not wearing an item of Highland dress; instead, his tartan adorns a long, loose-sleeved jacket.

In contrast to this pillar of the establishment, Richard Waitt's celebrated portrait of Kenneth Sutherland, Lord Duffus, depicts a prominent rebel who served as a naval officer during the rebellion of 1715. Painted in about 1712, the picture shows the nobleman in a belted plaid, wearing hunting colours. The pattern of the hose does not match the plaid and, in any case, neither can be linked with any certainty to a known sett. Typically for this period, tartan was more notable as a form of national dress than for its affiliation with specific clans.

THE 1715 REBELLION

Queen Anne died in 1714 and was succeeded by the Hanoverian George I. Immediately, Jacobites called for the return of the Old Pretender, James Francis Edward Stuart, the last son of James VII, who had already made one

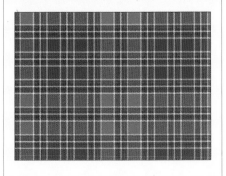

JACOBITE SETTS

For Jacobite supporters there was a tartan that they could wear as a badge of their protest. Over the years, at least six different Jacobite setts have been registered. The history of these tartans is difficult to gauge, as many of them are thought to date from a later era, when the Jacobite troubles were viewed with a sense of nostalgia. The one shown below, however, was created in 1707 and worn by particpants in the 1715 rebellion. It can still be worn as an alternative to a clan or district tartan.

▲ *A rare depiction of a Lowlander wearing tartan. Dalrymple's elaborate, tailored garment is very different from normal Highland dress.*

abortive bid for the throne in 1708. There were considerable doubts about George, both north and south of the border, and many Scots who had supported the Act of Union were by now thoroughly disillusioned with it.

This should have been the Old Pretender's ideal opportunity, but the campaign proved a shambles. Sporadic, poorly co-ordinated Jacobite uprisings were easily suppressed. The main force, under the leadership of the Earl of Mar, achieved some early successes, capturing Perth and fighting with distinction at the battle of Sheriffmuir. But James's lacklustre approach undermined the impetus of the rebellion. Fighting had actually broken out in August 1715, but he did not land on Scottish soil

until the end of December. Even then, his dour, fatalistic approach did little to inspire the Highlanders. Dubbed "old Mr Melancholy", in a speech to his officers he remarked: "It is no new thing to be unfortunate, since my whole life from my cradle has been a constant series of misfortunes." His army dwindled away and the rebellion petered out. Just six weeks after his arrival, the Old Pretender slunk back to France. He spent the rest of his life in exile, mainly in Rome, where the Pope continued to address him as the king of England.

AFTERMATH OF THE 1715 REBELLION

The government was not complacent about its success in quelling the 1715 rebellion. In many quarters it was readily accepted that the victory owed more to the incompetence of the enemy than to its own endeavours. As a result, attempts were made to pacify the Highlanders once and for all.

At this stage no measures were taken against the wearing of tartan, but efforts were made to undermine other aspects of the Highland way of life. There were renewed attempts to discourage the use of Gaelic. At the same time, religious bodies such as the Society for the Propagation of Christian Knowledge tried to persuade the clans to abandon their Catholic or Episcopalian beliefs in favour of the Presbyterianism that flourished in the Lowlands. The government also passed a Disarming Act although, in common with many other anti-Jacobite measures, it appears to have been enforced in a very half-hearted manner. Most of the Scots who handed over their weapons were loyal Lowlanders, while the rebels largely ignored the order.

▼ *Ruthven Barracks in Kingussie, built in 1718 to help suppress the Jacobites, were enlarged by George Wade in 1734.*

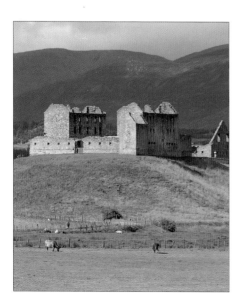

TRANSPORTATION TO THE COLONIES

Immediately after the 1715 rebellion, there were several executions and 19 peerages were forfeited. For other rebels, the standard penalty was transportation. There were fewer of these than is often supposed – probably no more than 800. The typical sentence was seven years, but many prisoners appear to have returned far sooner. James Mackintosh of Strathspey, for example, was indentured to serve a seven-year term in Virginia, but is known to have been back in Scotland

▲ *This map shows the roads and other improvements made by General Wade in the wake of the 1715 rebellion.*

less than two years after his departure. Nor was transportation always the terrible punishment it was designed to be. In 1717 Donald MacPherson, a Jacobite prisoner who had been taken to Maryland, sent back an optimistic message to his family in Inverness: "My master says to me, when I can speak like the folk here that I shall not be bidden to do nothing but make his blackamoors work; for decent folk here

ADOPTION OF THE KILT

Between the rebellions of 1715 and 1745, the kilt seems to have become established as the chief item of Highland dress. Before this, the belted plaid had been the preferred form of attire, particularly among soldiers and travellers, who used the garment as a blanket at night. Many theories have been put forward for the change in fashion, but the most likely reason was a military one.

The Earl Marischal began his account of the Jacobite rising by noting the flexibility of the plaid, "which the Highlanders tie about them in such a manner that it covers their thighs, and all their body when they please, but commonly it is fixed on their left shoulder, and leaves their right arm free." He went on to observe, however, how the clansmen tended to discard the plaid in battle. This was not necessarily a problem if a warrior was on the winning side. If he lost or was forced to retreat, on the other hand, then he had lost a vital piece of his equipment.

do not use to work but the first year after they come into the country; they speak all like the soldiers in Inverness."

Many Scottish prisoners fared even better. In the 1720s, Daniel Defoe noted: "So many of the Scots servants which go over to Virginia settle and thrive there, more than of the English…that if it goes on for many more years, Virginia may be rather called a Scots than an English plantation." Once such views became common, the deterrent value of transportation was somewhat reduced.

MILITARY ROADS

In fact, the only really effective measure taken by the English government in the wake of the 1715 rebellion lay

in the field of communications. In 1725 George Wade, Commander-in-Chief in Scotland, embarked on a massive building programme in the Highlands. Military roads were constructed in strategically important areas, most notably between Inverness and Fort William, from Inverness to Dunkeld, and between Crieff and Fort Augustus. Wade also built more than 40 bridges and transformed the royal barracks at Fort William, Fort Augustus and Fort George. These improved facilities enabled the English to police the Highlands far more effectively when the next rebellion occurred.

A ROMANTICIZED HERO

The Old Pretender was nowhere near colourful enough as a character to inspire the mythmakers of later generations, so instead the plaudits went to an outlaw named Rob Roy. His story is

▲ *Rob Roy, immortalized by Sir Walter Scott's romanticized version of his exploits, ambushes government troops.*

now mainly associated with the eponymous novel by Sir Walter Scott published in 1817, but Rob was earlier brought to the public's attention by Daniel Defoe's *Highland Rogue*, which appeared in 1729.

Rob belonged to the outlawed MacGregor clan, but spent much of his career masquerading as a Campbell. He operated at times as a *bona fide* livestock dealer and at other times as a cattle thief. His days as a Jacobite were equally ambiguous. He openly espoused the cause, acting as a guide for the rebels' army as they moved towards Sheriffmuir, but he took no part in the actual fighting. In spite of this, he was charged with treason and spent his later years as a fugitive.

THE JACOBITE REBELLION OF 1745

▲ *Bonnie Prince Charlie's triumphant entry into Edinburgh, where the Old Pretender was proclaimed king.*

Thirty years after the first main rebellion, the Jacobites rose again, making their final bid to place a Stuart on the throne. Technically, their candidate was still the Old Pretender, who had failed in the previous revolt, but he took no part in the campaign. Instead, it was his charismatic young son, Charles Edward Stuart, better known as Bonnie Prince Charlie or the Young Pretender, who championed the cause.

BONNIE PRINCE CHARLIE

Charles was born in exile in Rome, but travelled to France in 1744 in the hope of finding an ally. This was a logical move, since the French were involved in a major conflict against the English (the War of the Austrian Succession had broken out in 1740), and were rumoured to be planning an invasion. The French king was supportive at first, but abandoned the project when his fleet was dispersed by bad weather.

Undeterred, Charles made his own way to Scotland, landing initially at Eriskay in the Outer Hebrides before proceeding to Glenfinnan on the mainland, where he raised his father's standard. The early response was unpromising. After previous failures, many of the Highland chiefs were understandably reluctant to commit themselves, particularly as the Young Pretender did not have the backing of any foreign troops. However, Charles's great passion and commitment gradually convinced the western clans, most notably the Camerons and the MacDonalds, to rally behind him.

The initial signs were encouraging. The Jacobite army captured Perth and entered Edinburgh without opposition. This was swiftly followed by a significant victory over government forces at the battle of Prestonpans.

Buoyed by his early successes, Charles was anxious to press on into England, but already divisions were appearing within his own council. For some of the clansmen, the main object of the exercise had been achieved: the rightful Scottish king had been restored to his throne. The priority now was to defend it, until the French could launch their attack on England.

INVASION OF ENGLAND

This cautious approach was ignored, however, and in November 1745 Charles's army crossed the border. For a time, it seemed that the right decision had been made. The Scots encountered little resistance, and there was a mounting sense of panic further south. In London, one of the king's leading ministers, the Duke of Newcastle, admitted, "I look upon Scotland as gone," while George II (r.1727–60) gave orders for his most precious belongings to be transferred to the royal yacht in case he was forced to flee from his capital. Elsewhere, shops closed down as the city's inhabitants sought refuge in the countryside,

▼ *A highlight of the Jacobite campaign was the victory at Prestonpans, where the enemy commander was killed.*

and the Bank of England was almost ruined by a massive run on its funds.

In spite of this, there were growing concerns within the Scottish camp. As they marched south, they were gathering virtually no new recruits and some of their supporters were drifting away and heading back to Scotland. Increasingly, the realization dawned that they would be hopelessly outnumbered in England, where their dwindling force of around 5000 men would be pitted against as many as 30,000 Hanoverian troops. The army reached as far south as Derby, just 210km/130 miles from London, before these fears prompted them to halt their advance and turn around.

Charles was distraught at this decision, and historians have speculated ever since on what might have been. The retreat from Derby took much of the sting out of the Jacobites' campaign. The rebels did enjoy some further successes, particularly a minor victory over government troops in Falkirk, but once the threat of a genuine coup was removed the English were able to muster their forces and launch a decisive counterattack.

THE BATTLE OF CULLODEN

While the Jacobites were returning north, government ministers recalled some of their most experienced troops from the war in Flanders and placed them under the command of the king's ruthlessly efficient son, the Duke of Cumberland. He led them to Inverness, where the final encounter would take place. On nearby Culloden Moor the Jacobite forces were cut to pieces in a battle that lasted less than an hour. The barbaric behaviour of the Hanoverians, who slaughtered the wounded and anyone else in the vicinity in Highland dress, earned their commander the nickname "Butcher" Cumberland.

Charles made his escape from the battlefield, but spent the next five months living as a desperate fugitive, while royalist troops tried to hunt him down. In spite of the sizeable reward that was offered for his capture, none of his Highlanders betrayed him and he was eventually able to board a frigate bound for France. For the clansmen he left behind, the outlook was far bleaker. The authorities in London had been given a genuine scare by the Jacobite rising and were determined that the danger should never be repeated. Their solution was brutally simple – the destruction of the Highland clans and their entire way of life.

▼ *After the rout at Culloden, Prince Charles was forced into hiding, taking shelter wherever he could find it.*

A VOGUE FOR TARTAN

Amid the euphoria that followed Bonnie Prince Charlie's initial successes, there was a patriotic fashion for tartan clothes and artefacts. In Edinburgh, for example, merchants rushed to publicize their stocks of tartans "of the newest patterns". There was some irony in this, since Charles had not worn Highland dress thus far and had made his entry into the capital wearing red breeches and a green bonnet. Nevertheless, he did wear a kilt later in the campaign, as did his Lieutenant-General, Lord George Murray.

▼ *During his stay in Edinburgh, Charles held court at Holyrood.*

THE JACOBITE ROMANCE

No one knew it at the time, but the rebellion of 1745 was the swansong of the Jacobite movement. After the defeat at Culloden in 1746, Bonnie Prince Charlie spent his remaining years living as an exile, mainly in France and Italy. Eventually he became a disillusioned and embittered drunk, often confessing to his friends that he wished he had died on the battlefield alongside his loyal Highlanders.

In a later age, when the threat of Jacobitism was a distant memory, Scots looked back on this episode with an almost masochistic sense of nostalgia. It became a focus for national pride and as such inspired the creation of

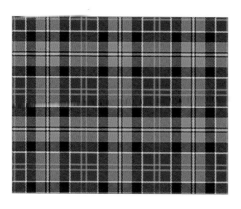

▲ *This Culloden is said to be based on a tartan worn by one of the prince's men.*

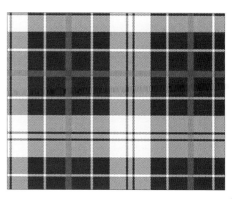

▲ *Culloden Red (dress) tartan is usually worn for dancing.*

▼ *Bonnie Prince Charlie raised his standard at Glenfinnan, calling on all Highlanders to join the Jacobite cause.*

numerous tartans. The designs relating to Bonnie Prince Charlie and Flora MacDonald, who aided his escape, fall into a similar category. Both have several setts named after them, and they were extremely popular during the revival period, when the careers of these two people were heavily romanticized. The designs were ostensibly based on historical artefacts, either old portraits or clothing that they were thought to have worn, but it is often hard to verify their authenticity.

CULLODEN TARTANS

Over the years, no fewer than 11 different Culloden tartans have been registered. Several of these are based, or purport to be based, on designs that were found on historical objects, such as clothing, portraits or furnishings. One is based on a set of bed-hangings found at Culloden House, which Charles had been using as his headquarters; the battle was fought just in front of the building. The most poignant example was apparently worn by one of the Highlanders who died on the field at Culloden. His identity is uncertain and the pattern is unlike any of the traditional clan setts, so it might almost be described as a tartan for the unknown soldier. Culloden tartans come into their own during events

▲ *As Bonnie Prince Charlie's saviour, Flora MacDonald – portrayed here by Richard Wilson – became the focal point of the Jacobite legend.*

staged on 16 April, the anniversary of the battle. This date is increasingly being chosen for celebrations as an alternative to St Andrew's Day (30 November) or Burns' Night (25 January), particularly for outdoor events, which are not well suited to winter weather. In Britain, for example, the National Tartan Day of 2000 (the so-called Maclennium) was held on the anniversary of Culloden.

BONNIE PRINCE CHARLIE AND TARTAN

In Charles's case there are signs that tartan was something of an afterthought. When he arrived in Scotland in 1745, he was dressed so soberly that one of his supporters mistook him for a minister, describing him as "a tall youth…in a plain black coat with a plain shirt not very clean and a cambrick stock fixed with a plain silver buckle…" It is likely, however, that the prince soon realized the propaganda value of wearing Highland dress, particularly when his Jacobite supporters presented him with a tartan outfit.

During his stay in the Highlands, Charles made further enquiries about this attire. The poet Alexander MacDonald, Flora MacDonald's cousin, later recalled how Charles had asked him if he found the garb chilly and if, when he was wrapped up tightly in his plaid at night, he was not concerned about being ambushed by an enemy. To the latter question, Alexander replied that "in such times of danger or during a war, we had a different method of using the plaid, that with one spring I could start to my feet with drawn sword and cock'd pistol in my hand, without being in the least encumber'd with my bedclothes."

The prince must have been convinced of the benefits, for he is on record as having worn Highland dress at various times during the 1745 rebellion. When he was hiding on Uist, for example, a certain Hugh MacDonald noted, "His dress was then a tartan short coat and vest of the same… a short kilt, tartan hose and Highland brogues, his upper coat being English cloth." Charles had been given this outfit by Lady Clanranald, but during the months that he lived as a fugitive his attire would normally have been far less conspicuous.

FLORA MACDONALD

Charles also spent some time dressed as a woman when he was aided in his escape from the English by Flora MacDonald, who disguised him as her Irish maid, Betty Burke. This was a hazardous undertaking, particularly since the prince seems to have been less than convincing in his part; one observer described him as "a very odd, muckle, ill-shapen up wife".

Flora's own life was every bit as colourful as that of her leader. After Charles's escape, she was arrested and taken to London where, even in captivity, she became something of a celebrity. Fanciful accounts were already circulating about her flight with the prince. In 1746, for example, an anonymous novel called *The Young Adventurer* created a great stir. This described how Alexis, "a shepherd of the first rank" (that is, Charlie), was defeated at the battle of Lachrymania, but was rescued by a beautiful girl called Heroica (Flora), who helped him escape to the island of Aetheria (Skye).

Flora was eventually released during an amnesty. She married and later emigrated to Wilmington, North Carolina, with her husband. There, she was greeted with great enthusiasm, as her fame had preceded her. Even so, a happy ending eluded her, for Flora's adopted homeland was soon caught up in its own struggle for independence. The couple were obliged to flee once again, taking refuge in Nova Scotia. There, they experienced a bleak, lonely winter, before returning home to Skye.

▼ *Later generations imagined a romance between Charles and Flora, though there is no evidence of this.*

AFTER CULLODEN

In England, the removal of the Jacobite threat was greeted with a mixture of elation and relief. The celebrations were extravagant. In London, a ballet called *Culloden*, which featured a deafening cannonade, was performed to packed houses at Sadler's Wells, while the Culloden Reel became the most popular dance of the day. For costume historians, though, the most intriguing contribution was a painting commissioned to mark the event – David Morier's *An Incident at Culloden*.

THE DISARMING ACT OF 1746

Away from the celebrations, the government showed a firm resolve to bring the Jacobite menace to an end. The Duke of Cumberland favoured a policy of transporting entire clans to the colonies, but in the end the authorities opted to tackle the problem at its roots. The Disarming Act of 1746 was the first of several decrees that struck at the very heart of Highland life. Along with a ban on the ownership of weapons, the heritable jurisdiction of the chiefs was abolished: Highland landowners

▲ *After Culloden, the authorities outlawed the wearing of tartan and all the accessories of Highland dress.*

▼ *Lucas' painting,* After Culloden: Rebel Hunting, *shows English soldiers arriving to arrest Jacobite supporters.*

HIGHLAND DRESS DURING THE JACOBITE ERA

An Incident at Culloden by the Swiss artist David Morier seems to confirm that no firm rules about the wearing of Highland dress had yet been established in the mid-18th century. Through the grace of his patron, the Duke of Cumberland, Morier was able to lend authenticity to his work by having a number of Jacobite prisoners brought to his studio to pose for him. They came from Southwark jail and the floating prison ships at Tilbury. Examples of plaids, kilts and trews are all pictured; no two men are dressed exactly alike and the eight principal clansmen in the painting wear 23 different tartans.

From other sources, it is clear that tartan was not used for identification purposes in battles of the period. Instead, Highlanders would usually rely on clan badges, often small plants, traditionally worn in their bonnets. Sometimes even this was insufficient, as members of the same clan might be fighting on different sides. Accordingly, at Culloden, clansmen wore a cockade in their hats – white for Charles, black for the English king.

had to accept English jurisdiction or forfeit their lands. This was a direct attack on clan loyalty, and many estates were forfeited.

HIGHLAND DRESS BANNED

Punitive restrictions on the wearing of Highland dress were introduced. "No man or boy shall, on any pretext whatever, wear or put on...the Plaid, Philabeg, or little Kilt, Trowse, Shoulder-belts, or any part whatever of men tried to exploit loopholes in the legislation. One youth, for instance, was held by soldiers for wearing a garment that resembled a kilt. He was later released, however, when it transpired that the offending article was stitched up the middle, in the manner of "the trousers worn by Dutch skippers".

CONTINUING PRIDE IN HIGHLAND DRESS

When the wearer was a known government supporter, the authorities would turn a blind eye, and as a result the practice of commissioning official portraits in Highland dress was unaffected. This trend was exemplified by William Mosman's striking depiction of John Campbell. Widely known as John Campbell of the Bank, he was a familiar figure in Edinburgh society. He enjoyed a long association with the Royal Bank of Scotland, which had been founded in 1727, serving as assistant secretary from 1732 and cashier from 1745, when he saved the bank's assets from the approaching Jacobite army by transferring them to the safety of Edinburgh Castle.

In spite of his firm allegiance to the Hanoverian cause, however, Campbell was proud of his Highland roots and, in particular, his descent from the house of Argyll. So, even though his portrait was commissioned from Mosman in 1749, not long after the new restrictions had come into force, he chose to be depicted in traditional Highland attire, in a belted plaid with a decorated cross-belt. He was also shown in the guise of a warrior, wearing both a claymore (a large double-edged broadsword) and a dagger, while a targe (a light shield) was displayed on the wall behind him.

The restrictions on Highland dress remained on the statute book for 35 years, until the law was eventually repealed in 1781. By this stage, the situation in the Highlands had been radically transformed.

▲ *John Campbell, of the Royal Bank of Scotland, was painted by William Mosman. His government connections enabled him to flout the ban on tartan.*

what peculiarly belongs to the Highland Garb; and no tartan or particoloured plaid or stuff shall be used for Great Coats or upper coats..." Bagpipes were also banned as "instruments of war". The penalties for ignoring these restrictions were severe. A first offence was punishable with six months' imprisonment, and any repeat entailed transportation to the colonies for a period of seven years.

ENFORCING THE ACT

The measures proved difficult to enforce, although the authorities certainly tried their best. A typical record states that, in 1749, Duncan Campbell and his son "were apprehended in Highland Cloaths by the moving Patrole and were confined in the Tolbooth [town jail] of Killin." Sometimes the letter of the law was applied to an absurd degree. On one occasion, for example, a black servant employed by Stewart of Appin was arrested and imprisoned, simply because his master had kitted him out in tartan livery. Inevitably, some clans-

THE START OF SCOTTISH EMIGRATION

The punitive measures introduced in the wake of Culloden helped to bring about lasting change in the Highlands. For many clansmen, it seemed that life in their native land was no longer a viable option and they decided to try their fortunes elsewhere. In doing so, they were following in a long tradition.

Scottish emigration had begun long before the Jacobite problem arose. The overwhelming reason for this was poverty. In the Highlands, in particular, many people lived barely at subsistence level, rearing livestock or growing meagre crops. When the latter failed, as they did in 1572, 1587 and 1595, there were severe famines. From the early years of the 17th century many Scots also decided to leave their homeland due to the religious divisions that were starting to tear their country apart.

SOLDIERS OF FORTUNE AND SCHOLARS

From the outset, emigrant Scots distinguished themselves in a variety of fields. They were probably best known as soldiers: Scottish mercenaries became renowned for their courage and dependability throughout Europe. Their most common destinations were Scandinavia and France, with which Scots maintained the "auld alliance" against their common enemy, the English. These connections can be seen in the evolution of French names such as De Gaulle (from Dougal), De Lisle (Leslie), or Le Clerc (Clark).

Other Scots made their mark in Europe as scholars or clerics. The most celebrated examples of the former are probably the philosophers Duns Scotus (*c*.1266–1308), who taught at Oxford, Paris and Cologne, and Michael Scott the Wizard (*c*.1160–*c*.1235), who worked in Paris, Padua and Rome. In later years, so many Scots chose this route out of their native land that, in

the 16th century, the Collège d'Ecosse at the University of Paris catered for 400 Scottish scholars.

COMMERCIAL TRAVELLERS IN EASTERN EUROPE

In Poland, meanwhile, the Scots became better known in the field of commerce. They ranged from bankers and merchants to the *kramers*, or pedlars, who set up booths in many Polish towns, selling knives, scissors and woollen goods. In 1616 the traveller William Lithgow noted that 30,000 Scots families were living in Poland. It is hard to gauge the accuracy of this figure, although it is certainly true that the Polish authorities were concerned

▲ *Many Highlanders sought their fortune as mercenaries, acquiring a reputation for courage and ferocity.*

about the number of Scottish youths who resorted to begging. As in France, the trend can be confirmed from the prevalence of names such as Czamer (from Chalmers), Zutter (Soutar), Zlot (Scott) and Grim (Graham).

NOVA SCOTIA

After James VI's accession to the English throne as James I in 1603, Scots became more involved in the process of colonization. The king extended the policy of creating "plantations" in Ireland, although many colonists preferred to look further afield, to the opportunities opening up in the Americas.

The first Scottish venture of note in the New World was launched by Sir William Alexander, Earl of Stirling. In 1621, he acquired large tracts of land in Canada and hatched the scheme of creating a new Scotland, imitating the settlements of New Holland and New England. The colony was accordingly named Nova Scotia. Early attempts at establishing the settlement proved disappointing, however, even after Alexander penned a pamphlet entitled *An Encouragement to Colonies*.

Gradually, the project degenerated into little more than a money-making scheme, for in 1625 Alexander created his Nova Scotia baronetcies. This enabled Scottish entrepreneurs to purchase a title for cash and a promise to provide a certain number of settlers. Most of the investors had no intention of travelling to Nova Scotia, however, and in due course the undertaking to provide new settlers was replaced by an additional fee. In all, 64 baronetcies

▼ *Followers of the philosopher Duns Scotus were labelled "dunces" by critics of their unorthodox views.*

were created, many of them held by the chiefs of major clans. The colony itself soon passed to the French, and it was only in the 18th century that Scottish settlers began to arrive there in significant numbers.

THE EXPEDITION TO PANAMA

The driving force behind another, disastrous, enterprise was the financier William Paterson (1658–1719). As the founder of the Bank of England, he readily found backers for his project – a settlement on the Darien Isthmus in Panama that could serve as a trading base for both the Atlantic and the Pacific. Paterson's scheme was set up in 1695 as a joint venture between English and Scottish investors. However, the project was effectively sabotaged by William II, who had his own reasons for wishing to undermine any Scottish enterprise, and by the wealthy East India Company.

Following the intervention of these parties, the English investors withdrew, leaving the Scots to finance the entire risk on their own. Undeterred, Paterson pressed ahead, sailing out with the first batch of settlers in 1698. They grandly renamed the area New Caledonia and founded a base at Fort St Andrew. Unaware of the malarial conditions, many of the settlers succumbed to fever, while the remainder were soon overrun by Spanish forces. By 1700 the

▲ *This wooden church was erected in the 18th century by Scottish settlers at Pictou, in Nova Scotia.*

entire project had been abandoned, with considerable loss of life and money. The failure of the expedition was blamed on the English, although ironically it also increased calls for the union of the two countries, since it was evident that Scotland had more to gain by co-operating, rather than competing, with its powerful neighbour.

▼ *Herman Moll's 1699 map of New Caledonia relates to the attempt to found a Scottish colony in Panama.*

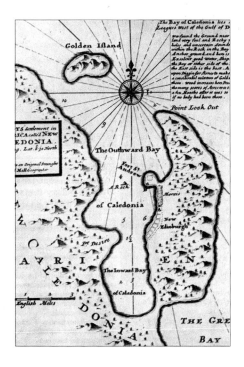

EMIGRATION IN THE 18TH CENTURY

The rate of emigration from the Highlands increased dramatically in the 18th century. Many of the expatriates eventually made new homes for themselves in the New World, taking with them the most important elements of their native culture.

POLITICAL DEPORTATIONS

Many of these emigrants were sent abroad under compulsion. Exile "beyond the seas" had been a standard punishment since the 17th century, particularly for those Scots who rebelled against the government. This form of transportation was usually for a fixed period (seven or 14 years were common terms), but many of the deportees remained in America after their release, and went on to become valued citizens. In Boston, for example, some of the Scots who had been expelled during the Civil War were responsible for setting up the Scots Charitable Society, which was founded in the city in 1657 and was the first organization of its kind in America.

TRANSPORTATION OF CONVICTED CRIMINALS

Certain types of criminal were also candidates for transportation. This kind of punishment was operated in a very

▼ *The Scots Charitable Society held many of its meetings at the historic Green Dragon Inn in Boston.*

haphazard fashion by the English, until the government introduced the Transportation Act of 1718, which regulated the system and made it far more profitable. Similar penalties were meted out in Scottish courts, although technically the latter had no legal right to send convicts to English colonies prior to the Act of Union of 1707. Instead, felons were banished "furth [outside] of the kingdom".

In Scotland, transportation was mainly reserved for capital offences, although prisoners could also petition for this sentence if they feared that the alternative might be worse. As a result, surviving records of Scottish transports indicate a wide variety of criminals, ranging from murderers and rapists to horse-thieves and counterfeiters. The system was open to abuse. Until heritable jurisdictions were abolished in 1748, after the battle of Culloden, clan chiefs enjoyed the right to banish certain offenders. Sometimes, however, prisoners were allowed to escape, if this suited clan interests; conversely, troublesome tenants were evicted from their land and transported purely on the basis of trumped-up charges.

Scotland deported considerably fewer of its criminals than either England or Ireland and, for this reason, the actual

▲ *An engraving of 1770 shows Scottish convicts shackled together, awaiting transportation to North America.*

process of transportation worked less efficiently. There were fewer ships dealing with this kind of cargo, and most captains were interested only in taking able-bodied young men who could readily be sold on as indentured servants. Many women and elderly people faced the prospect of lengthy delays, confined in prison, before they could actually begin their sentence. In 1734, for example, a female convict, Janet Jamieson, complained that "no merchants that traded to America would undertake to Transport her, unless she could pay her passage". Similarly, in 1729, a William Lauder bemoaned the fact that he had been held for three years in a tolbooth (jail), since he was old and "not fit for any Service in the Plantations".

A NEW LIFE

There was far greater Scottish participation in the more conventional forms of emigration, which mushroomed after 1700. New Jersey, which became a Crown Colony in 1702, was a popular destination for Scots, most notably in 1684, when almost 300 set sail from

WEARING HIGHLAND DRESS

Wherever they ventured, the clansmen made a point of displaying their Highland dress. In 1736, when Governor Oglethorpe of Georgia came to meet the Scots defending the frontier against the Spanish, he found them dressed in plaids and kilts and, in a diplomatic show of solidarity, agreed to try the outfit himself. Native Americans were fascinated by the bright colours of the tartans, which were so different from most European attire. Writing in the 1750s, David Stuart of Garth noted, "When the Highlanders landed, they were caressed by all ranks and orders of men, but more particularly by the Indians. On the march to Albany, the Indians flocked from all quarters to see the strangers who, they believed, were of the same extraction as themselves, and therefore received them as brothers."

home. The new settlement of Georgia, founded in 1732, attracted many Highlanders, as did the Cape Fear River area of North Carolina. In the latter, in particular, emigrant Scotsmen swiftly made their mark. There were also substantial Scottish settlements in the Mohawk and Upper Hudson Valleys in New York, and further north at Prince Edward Island and Pictou in Nova Scotia.

Even though the idea of a new start may have been tempting, the decision to emigrate was always a momentous step. Quite apart from the uncertainties surrounding their new home, the travellers were often exploited by unscrupulous speculators and ships' captains, and the voyage itself could be hazardous. The hazards were typified by the terrible journey endured by some 200 Scots who in 1773

▲ *Sentimental emigration scenes, such as John Watson Nicol's* Lochaber No More, *were a popular Victorian theme.*

set out from Ullapool aboard the *Hector*. The ship, which belonged to two Englishmen, departed with insufficient provisions, so that after two months at sea the drinking water was green and the only food was mouldy oatcakes. During the trip, 18 children died of smallpox or dysentery. At Newfoundland, the ship was driven back by gales, adding a further two weeks to the journey, so when the settlers finally arrived in Nova Scotia it was too late in the season to prepare the land or plant crops for the following year. Despite all this, they went ashore proudly, led by their piper and wearing the plaids and tartans that were still banned in their native land.

▼ *The* Hector *is a replica of the ship that carried many Scots to Canada. It was launched at Pictou in 2000.*

TARTAN REVIVAL

THE BAN WAS REPEALED IN 1782, BUT IT WAS GEORGE IV'S STATE VISIT TO SCOTLAND THAT REALLY SIGNALLED A CHANGE IN PUBLIC OPINION. ALMOST OVERNIGHT, HIGHLAND DRESS BECAME HUGELY FASHIONABLE, AS EVERY CLAN RUSHED TO VERIFY THEIR TARTAN.

THE REPEAL OF THE BAN

In the summer of 1782, the restrictions that had been placed on the wearing of tartan after the battle of Culloden in 1746 were finally removed. Once the bill had gained royal assent, a proclamation went out around the Highlands affirming "to every man, young and old…that they may after this put on and wear the Trews, the little Kilt, the Doublet and Hose, along with the Tartan Kilt, without fear of the Law of the Land or the jealousy of enemies…"

Earlier in the year, a delegation from the Highland Society of London had approached James Graham, the future 3rd Duke of Montrose, to ask if he might raise the matter in official circles. This was a shrewd choice. Graham was a member of parliament in England, but he came from a family that had a proud tradition of supporting the Stuart cause, and he duly introduced a bill calling for the repeal of the old Disarming Act. This provoked little controversy and the legislation was swiftly passed.

News of the lifting of the ban was greeted warmly by many Scots. The Gaelic poet Duncan MacIntyre, for example, composed a "Song to the Highland Garb", rejoicing in the occasion. Nevertheless, the overall response was surprisingly muted. In many quarters, there was a feeling that it was no longer an issue of major significance.

There were several reasons for this. In England, the most important factor was that the threat of another Jacobite rebellion had long since receded. After Culloden Prince Charles, the Young Pretender, had travelled around France and Spain before eventually settling in Italy. He gained no promises of support during the course of his wanderings in these Catholic countries, and gradually his own followers began to lose faith in

Previous pages: Inverlochy Castle.

him. He was also heavily criticized in 1752, when he took Clementina Walkinshaw as his mistress. Her sister was a lady-in-waiting at the Hanoverian court, and there were many who regarded her as a spy.

The final turning point for the Jacobite movement occurred in 1766, with the death of the Old Pretender, Charles's father. Significantly, neither the Pope nor the king of France acknowledged Charles's right to the British throne. Instead, he remained in exile and, by the 1780s, was a forgotten man. When he died in 1788, his brother, Henry Benedict (1725–1807), last male heir of the Stuart line, made no claim to the throne. He had already pursued a successful career in the Church, becoming a cardinal in 1747.

A LOST CRAFT

Among the Scots themselves there was a more poignant reason for the mixed response to the repeal of the ban, namely that the measures drawn up in the Disarming Act had worked only

▲ *David Wilkie's* Distraining for Rent *(1815) illustrates the plight of many crofters as rents rose dramatically.*

too well. Although there had been some notable attempts to evade the regulations, most people had simply conformed. This situation could not easily be reversed in 1782, because most Highlanders had more pressing problems to deal with. As Dr Johnson noted, "The same poverty that made it difficult for them to change their clothing, hinders them now from changing it back." Sir John Sinclair's *Old Statistical Account* (1799) included an entry from Kincardine that lamented the loss of the old cloth-making skills: "Deprived of the pleasure of seeing their husbands, sons, and favourites, in that elegant drapery, emulation died, and they became contented with manufacturing the wool in the coarsest and clumsiest manner…"

The truth of this account is confirmed by the problems that later researchers encountered when they were trying to trace the early development of tartan. They discovered that the old dyeing methods had largely been forgotten, and that the pattern-sticks described by the historian Martin Martin at the end of the 17th century had all been lost. At the time of the tartan revival, both chiefs and clansmen found it hard to establish which designs their ancestors had actually worn.

SHIFTING RELATIONSHIPS

One of the key strategies of the Hanoverian government had been to undermine the strength of the Highland clan system by weakening the links between the chief and his followers. They tried to do this by confiscating traditional clan lands and revoking heritable jurisdiction. Some of the estates were later restored but, even so, the parental nature of the relationship between the chief and his

▼ *In* The Last of the Clan *(1865), by Thomas Faed, a forlorn old clansman watches his family leave home forever.*

clansmen had begun to wane. In its place, there was a growing sense of commercialism, in which the chief assumed the status of a landlord rather than a patriarch.

LAND CLEARANCES

This subtle shift of attitudes became significant as the prevailing economic conditions deteriorated. From the

▲ *The remains of crofters' cottages at Moidart: the clearances left large tracts of the Highlands virtually uninhabited.*

1760s, rents began to rise dramatically and landowners looked for more profitable ways of managing their assets. In practical terms, this often meant clearing the land of its tenants and sub-tenants, in order to exploit its full commercial value. The earliest attempts to do this, dating back to the 1730s, had been greeted with horror and threats of prosecution. As the 18th century went on, however, increasing numbers of landlords began to adopt this solution.

In many cases, the small crofting communities, with their scattered strips of arable land, were replaced by huge sheep farms. The industry was scarcely new in Scotland, but it underwent great changes in the 18th century. Different breeds, such as the black-faced Linton and the Cheviot, were introduced. These were hardy enough to survive the rigours of a Highland winter, and the combined value of their meat and their wool made them more profitable than cattle. The drawback was that they required a great deal of grazing land and, in many parts of the Highlands, they gradually began to displace the poorer clansmen.

A NEW IMAGE FOR THE HIGHLANDS

While the plight of many Highlanders grew steadily worse during the course of the 18th century, their public image began to change out of all recognition. As the threat of a Jacobite invasion faded, the history of the movement was rewritten, presenting a sanitized and romantic view of events.

Fictionalized versions of the 1745 rebellion soon began to captivate the public. The most popular of these was *The Young Adventurer* or, to give it its cumbersome full title, *The Young Adventurer, containing a particular account of all that happened to a certain person during his wanderings in the North, from his memorable defeat in April 1746 to his final escape on the 19th of September in the same year.* This was

▶ Bonnie Prince Charlie enters Edinburgh, *by John Leigh Pemberton, focuses on the glamour of the '45.*

Tartan featured heavily among the popular songs of the 18th century, largely, possibly, because "tartan plaidie" offered a convenient rhyme for "Highland Laddie". Even so, it soon came to acquire romantic connotations, which made it preferable to more costly materials, as the narrator of the following verse confirms:

A painted Room and Silken Bed
May please a Lawland Laird and Lady,
But I can kiss and be as glad
Behind a Bush in's Highland Plaidy.

Many songs took this a stage further, using the conceit of a lady exchanging her costly garments for the more romantic attire of the Highlands as a symbol of a passionate love affair:

TARTANA

Now She's cast off her silken Gowns
that she wear'd in the Lowland,
And she's up to the Highland Hills
to wear Gowns of Tartain.

Allan Ramsay (1686–1758), the poet who had done so much to popularize the Highland Laddie songs, wrote a lyric in praise of "Tartana". In it, he described how the warriors and shepherds throughout old Caledonia had decked themselves out in colourful plaids. Similarly, it is significant that one of the many accounts of the Young Pretender's adventures gave the prince the pseudonym of "Young Tartan".

▶ Tartana *(c.1845) by J.C. Armytage: the craze for all things tartan lasted well into the 19th century.*

fashionable reading not just in Britain but throughout much of western Europe, following its translation into French, Spanish and Italian.

POPULAR SONGS

The trend was not confined to novels, but was also evident in the popular songs of the period. Both the Jacobites and the Whigs (supporters of the Hanoverians) had produced songs that reflected their very different viewpoints. Alongside these were songs about the contemporary Highlander stereotype – the so-called "Highland Laddie" – who displayed very contradictory qualities. On the one hand, he was a violent and uncouth figure, yet at the same time his primitive qualities earned him a great reputation as a lover, who was more attractive to the English or Lowland ladies than their own refined menfolk.

After the Jacobite uprising, the political and romantic themes of such songs gradually merged, as Prince Charles, the Young Pretender, became increasingly associated with the Highland Laddie. In effect, he embarked upon his transformation into the romanticized figure of Bonnie Prince Charlie. As the memory of the rebellion receded and Jacobite sympathies became a picturesque reminder of the past, the underlying message of these songs began to change. Increasingly, the rebels seemed to conjure up a national spirit that could be appreciated by all Scots, whether Lowlanders or Highlanders. Tartan was tied in with this trend.

HEROIC BESTSELLERS

In 1760, James Macpherson (1736–96) published his *Fragments of Ancient Poetry Collected in the Highlands of Scotland and Translated from the Gaelic or Erse Language*. According to the author, these verses were part of a heroic epic that had been composed in the 3rd century AD by a Caledonian bard called Ossian. The *Fragments*

aroused considerable interest in Edinburgh literary circles, and Macpherson was provided with the funds to continue his research into this field. The author duly travelled around some of the remoter parts of the Highlands and the Western Isles, returning with sufficient material for two further collections of verse – *Fingal, An Ancient Epic Poem...composed by Ossian, the Son of Fingal* (1761) and *Temora, An Ancient Epic Poem in Eight Books* (1763).

The response to Macpherson's books was phenomenal. They were bestsellers, both in Britain and throughout much

▼ *The Ossian poems inspired romantic visions of a Celtic past such as Ingres'* Dream of Ossian *(1813).*

of Europe. Goethe, Schubert and Schiller all sang their praises, while Napoleon owned an edition. The narrative was adapted into plays, operas and paintings.

Macpherson's verses recounted the adventures of a legendary race of giant warriors who had once ruled over the wilds of Caledonia, but the stories themselves were less important than the image they represented. The picture of a noble race of savages appealed to the sensibilities of the budding Romantic movement, and helped to promote a revival of interest in Celtic matters. From a Scottish standpoint, the poems, if genuine, meant that the country could lay claim to an ancient cultural tradition; a tradition that, very pointedly, England could not match.

THE HIGHLAND SOCIETIES

The Jacobite songs and the poems ascribed to Ossian presented a romantic view of the Highlands, mysterious and glamorous, which became known as "Highlandism". For all its attractions, though, it was in many respects a false vision, and one that the area has been slow to shake off. Yet, at the very time that Highlandism was emerging, attempts were also being made to define and preserve the true origins of Highland culture.

The pioneers in this field were the Highland Society of London, founded in 1778, and its sister organization, the Highland Society of Scotland, established six years later. The structure of these bodies was most unusual. In part, they were economic think-tanks that aimed to improve the financial state of the Highlands by promoting modernization. Among other things, they called for improvements in the fishing and farming industries, the upgrading of transport links, and the establishment of new towns and villages.

PROMOTING HIGHLAND CULTURE

Alongside these commercial activities, the societies also took a keen interest in the language and the arts of the Highlands. Their most illustrious achievement in this respect, perhaps, was the creation of a long-running piping competition, which the London branch established in 1781. In addition, both societies took a keen interest in the state of the Gaelic language. Their prognosis was hardly encouraging, for they believed it had "found a refuge in the Highlands of Scotland as a sanctuary in which it might expire". Even so, they commissioned a Gaelic dictionary, which was published in 1828.

The societies' other main task in this field was to organize an enquiry into the authenticity of James Macpherson's

Ossianic verses. This had remained a controversial issue, largely because the author had been so coy about revealing the Gaelic sources he had used. For many, it seemed suspicious that the material was so close to the stories in the Irish Fenian cycle, which featured several of the same characters. The investigating committee of the Highland Society considered the matter for several years before eventually producing a 300-page report, which was published in 1805. Its conclusions were disappointingly non-committal: it found that Macpherson had used some material of genuine antiquity, but had altered it dramatically, changing the names, places and mood of his Gaelic source and filling in the gaps with long passages of his own invention. Significantly, the committee's report had no effect whatsoever on the popularity of the books.

TARTAN SURVEY

In 1815, the Highland Society of London embarked on one of the earliest and most valuable surveys of tartan. Anxious to discover just how many named clan tartans were in circulation, they asked the chief of each clan for a

▲ As Highland travel became easier, artists sought out picturesque sights such as this view of Inverness (1779).

sample of their traditional sett. The chiefs were also encouraged to authenticate the sample by adding their seal and signature to it.

The project went ahead smoothly and, by 1816, 74 different specimens had been collected and identified. In some cases, they are the earliest known examples of the tartan in question. The Galbraith, Gow and Mackinnon setts all fall within this category. The survey often highlighted the inconsistent manner in which tartans were still being used. The Galbraith design, for example, is identical to that used by the Russells, the Hunters and the Mitchells, and it is not clear who first adopted the pattern. Similarly, the Highland Society's sample of the Mackinnon tartan features a light blue stripe that distinguishes it from other early versions of the sett. Most revealing of all, perhaps, was the comment that came back from many of the chiefs, confessing that they did not know their clan tartan and asking for help in ascertaining what it should be.

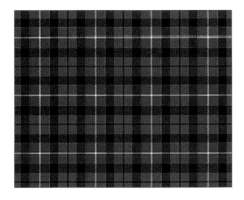

▲ *The Galbraith tartan is identical to the Russells, Hunters and Mitchells.*

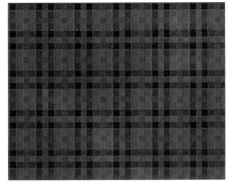

▲ *The Gow tartan, one of the earliest identified setts.*

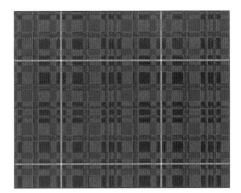

▲ *The Mackinnon tartan, with its distinguishing blue stripe.*

EARLY TOURISTS

While bodies such as the Highland Society were analysing the living conditions of the far north for the benefit of their learned members, the area was also becoming more familiar to the public at large. The road links that General Wade had constructed in the 1720s along the main arteries of the Highlands meant that travel through the region, while still hazardous, was considerably easier than in the past.

▼ *Fingal's Cave, discovered in 1772, rapidly became a source of inspiration for Romantic musicians and artists.*

This encouraged more outsiders to visit the area, many of whom published accounts of their journeys.

Prominent among these tourists was the naturalist Sir Joseph Banks, who travelled to see the geological wonders on the isle of Staffa. The highlight here was Fingal's Cave, which took its name from a hero in Macpherson's *Ossian*. A Welshman, Thomas Pennant, found the Highlands "almost as little known to its southern brethren as Kamchatka".

The most celebrated visitors were Dr Johnson and James Boswell. They travelled through the Highlands and islands in 1773, later recording their

impressions in two famous books. Johnson's *Journey to the Western Isles* appeared in 1775, and Boswell's *Journal of a Tour to the Hebrides* a decade later. The doctor's notorious dislike of the Scots hardly presented a balanced view of the local culture. Nevertheless, his colourful descriptions of the Highlanders and their customs brought the region to life for many British people, who had regarded it as a wild and savage place.

▼ *Despite Dr Johnson's forebodings, he and Boswell were treated hospitably during their tour of the Highlands.*

GEORGE IV'S VISIT TO SCOTLAND

Although tartan was being worn again by the early years of the 19th century, a full-scale revival had not yet begun. This occurred almost overnight following George IV's official visit to Edinburgh in 1822, which was of considerable political significance as it marked the first occasion on which a Hanoverian monarch had set foot on Scottish soil. It was also an important moment for advocates of Highland dress, since tartan featured heavily in the proceedings and the king himself donned a kilt during the celebrations.

After years of living in the shadow of his father, George III, and having spent almost ten years as regent (1811–20) after he was deemed insane, George IV (r.1820–30) finally became king at the age of 42. Already notorious for his extravagance and dandyism, he spent a year planning his summer coronation in 1821 and, having developed a taste for lavish ceremonial,

▼ *George IV travelled to Scotland on his yacht the* Royal George, *this painting depicts his arrival at Leith.*

decided to follow this up with a royal progress through his kingdom. The focal point of his visit to Scotland was to be an affirmation of the union between England and Scotland, a symbolic reconciliation between the two countries, following the Jacobite uprisings in the previous century.

SIR WALTER SCOTT'S PAGEANT
The details of the visit were put in the hands of the Lord Provost of Edinburgh, who in turn invited the novelist and poet Sir Walter Scott to manage the affair. Scott's love of pageantry and tradition made him the ideal choice. He had already attended George's coronation and conducted detailed research into the subject of royal progresses for his latest novel, *Kenilworth*, which had been published in 1821. Once preparations got under way, Scott's house in Castle Street, Edinburgh, became a hive of activity, prompting the author himself to remark, "This town has been a scene of such giddy tumult...I am astonished that I did not fever in the midst of it."

TARTAN AS A SYMBOL OF UNITY
The amount of tartan on show during King George IV's visit to Scotland impressed most people. One observer noted, "It seemed that the Highland clans with sword and pistol at their belts, bagpipes playing, and tartans waving, had come to re-occupy the capital, as in the '45...a tartan fit had come upon the city and...marched out to welcome the royal visitor." Scott would not have been pleased at this mention of the Jacobite uprising of 1745, since these were the very associations that he wished to dispel. In the past, tartan had been a mark of rebellion, but now it was to be a symbol of unity and lineage.

Scott wanted the royal visit to stress the cultural independence of his nation and to make the recently rediscovered Honours of Scotland – the royal regalia consisting of the crown, sceptre and

▲ *The royal regalia, known as the Honours of Scotland, were the focal point of many celebrations during George IV's state visit to Edinburgh.*

sword of state – a centrepiece of the event. They had been locked away in Edinburgh Castle after the Act of Union in 1707 and forgotten until Scott had made an official enquiry as to their whereabouts. Scott was present at their rediscovery in a padlocked oak chest in 1818.

TARTAN TAKES CENTRE STAGE

Walter Scott also insisted that kilts, tartans and pipes should play a prominent role and invited many of the leading clan chiefs to play a part in the proceedings. Not all of them came but a steady stream of "wild Highlanders" thronged to see him, often "completely armed so that the house rang with broadswords and targets and pipes from daybreak to sunset".

The response was also sufficient to create a genuine shortage in the supply of tartan, which led some of the guests to take drastic measures. The Sutherland Highlanders, for example, even persuaded a weaving firm to part with an entire batch of uniforms destined for the Black Watch.

The twin notions of ancestry and tradition were emphasized at every juncture during George's visit. After

disembarking at the port of Leith, the king was led on a triumphal procession through the streets of Edinburgh, where banners proclaimed: "Welcome to the land of your ancestors," and "Descendant of the immortal Bruce, thrice Welcome." When the king appeared dressed in a kilt of Royal Stewart tartan at a sumptuous levée in Holyrood Palace, a deliberate link was forged between the Jacobite Pretenders of the past and the present-day legitimate monarch.

The clans played an even greater role during a second procession, in which George paraded, accompanied by the royal regalia, from Holyrood to

Edinburgh Castle. On this occasion, the king was attended by the Drummonds, the MacDonells, the Sutherland Highlanders, the Breadalbane Men and the MacGregors, who were all attired in their tartan finery. The ceremony was marred by a heavy downpour, but the king was sufficiently impressed to remark to one of the organizers: "What a fine sight. I had no conception there was such a scene in the world...and the people are as beautiful and extraordinary as the scene."

During the remainder of his stay, George reviewed his Scottish troops, attended a service at St Giles's Cathedral and was guest of honour at several balls. One of his final and most enjoyable duties was a visit to the Theatre Royal, to see a dramatized version of *Rob Roy*, one of Sir Walter Scott's most popular novels. This was a fitting tribute to the man who, more than any other, had ensured the success of the royal visit and who, in the process, had almost single-handedly revived the fortunes of tartan.

▼ *Painted by John Ewbank, this panoramic view illustrates the pageantry of the reception that greeted the king in 1822.*

SIR WALTER SCOTT

George IV's visit to Scotland in 1822 produced a mixed response from Scottish commentators. Most were impressed by the sheer spectacle of the occasion, though a few dismissed it as a masquerade. One pundit, for example, summed up the entire event as "Sir Walter's Celtified Pageantry". Even Scott's sternest critics, however, could hardly deny that the author had done much to foster a new public image for his country. This image was built up over the course of his career, and should not be linked exclusively to the royal visit.

Walter Scott was born in Edinburgh, but spent many of his formative years in the Borders, where he became entranced by the area's history and developed a fascination with the past

▲ *As the self-appointed guardian of Scottish tradition, no one did more to promote the revival of tartan than Sir Walter Scott.*

that would dominate his entire life. As a youth, he had hoped to become a soldier, but a childhood illness left him with a permanent limp and effectively ended this ambition. Instead, he followed his father into the law. The work seemed like pure drudgery to him, although it was not without relevance to his writing career. The Jacobite rebellion was still a living memory for the older generation and many of Scott's cases dealt with the lingering effects of the uprising – issues such as forfeited estates and disputed inheritances. As part of his job, the young

man even met a few of the conflict's survivors. Inevitably, this stirred his imagination, giving him much of the material that he would later recycle into his stories

POET AND NOVELIST

As he embarked on his literary pursuits, Scott initially made his mark as a poet. *The Lay of the Last Minstrel* (1805) brought him his first real taste of success, and was swiftly followed by a number of other verse romances. Scott ploughed this furrow for almost a decade, until the rise of Byron persuaded him to try his hand at other genres, culminating in the publication of the novel *Waverley* (1814), his ground-breaking venture into prose. The book was published under a pseudonym – because Scott was worried about jeopardizing his legal career – and was an immediate success, going through four editions in its first year.

Waverley tells the story of a naive young English soldier, who comes from a Hanoverian background but also has an uncle with Jacobite sympathies. When he is posted to Scotland during the rebellion, he comes into contact with some of his uncle's friends and rapidly becomes embroiled in the rising itself. These political complications are mirrored in the hero's private life: he falls in love with the sister of a Jacobite leader, but is eventually saved by a devoted admirer, who comes from a far less dangerous background.

The underlying theme of *Waverley* is one that Scott returned to again and again – a divided Scotland. This division centred on the choice between the emotional pull of the country's Celtic past and the modernizing influences that appeared to be its future. The dichotomy was apparent in Scott's own nature. In his heart, he was a Jacobite, captivated by the old culture of the

Highlands, but in his head he was a Unionist, aware that the links with England were likely to bring his country prosperity and influence.

In part, the book's impact was due to the sheer originality of the form, for with *Waverley* Scott effectively invented the historical novel. The combination of the colourful setting, the adventure and the love interest captured the spirit of the times, appealing to devotees of the Romantic movement then in full flood. The author wasted no time in exploiting this trend, producing a series of novels that dealt with evocative periods in Scottish history. Prominent among them were *Rob Roy* (1817), which revolves around the escapades of a famous outlaw, and *Redgauntlet* (1824), which focuses on an imaginary third Jacobite rebellion, in which Bonnie Prince Charlie returns to take up the struggle once more.

PRESERVING HIGHLAND CULTURE

Scott's attachment to the past led him to try to preserve its most important features. His determination to revive the popularity of tartan is a memorable example of this, but the same instincts

▲ *Jeanie Deans wears a tartan shawl in a scene from Scott's novel,* The Heart of Midlothian *(1818).*

also prompted him to record the old ballads and folk tales of the Borders before they disappeared. When he became rich, he also felt driven to build up a collection of historical knick-knacks. Among the relics preserved in his home at Abbotsford are a lock of Bonnie Prince Charlie's hair, a purse and *skean dhu* (stocking dagger) that belonged to Rob Roy and, most poignant of all, a piece of oatcake found on the body of a Highlander killed at Culloden.

THE SCOTTISH FASHION

Through the medium of his books, Scott managed to transmit his enthusiasm for the traditional culture to the rest of Europe. His novels were enormously popular throughout the continent, and they inspired a vogue

◄ *A passion for Scottish styles swept Europe, and this tartan dress appeared on a French fashion plate in 1826.*

for all things Scottish. The most visible evidence of this influence was the craze for tartan, which extended far beyond the borders of Scotland. In France, for example, fashion designers incorporated strips of tartan into their latest creations and there was a veritable passion for *la mode écossaise*.

In later years, this was sometimes seen as a cause for regret. Scott has often been described as the architect of Highlandism; more than anyone else, he was responsible for the way that Highland culture and history was reinvented and repackaged for the popular market. This gave Scotland a much higher profile within Europe, as well as a heightened sense of national identity, but it also laid the foundations of a stereotyped view of the country that persisted into modern times.

TARTAN AS A COSTUME

In its original form, Highland dress had developed as a simple and practical outfit, which was perfectly adapted to the needs of the people who wore it. During the period of the tartan revival, however, this approach no longer prevailed. Many of the people who donned kilts or plaids regarded them either as examples of national costume, or else as items of fashionable wear. Accordingly, the appearance of the garments seemed far more important than any notions of historical accuracy.

FANCY DRESS

The most extreme example of this attitude was provided by George IV. In his youth, he acquired a reputation as a dandy and, long before he ever set foot in Scotland, he had developed a fondness for Highland dress. In 1789, when he was 27 years old, he and his two brothers were given Scottish outfits and received instruction in the wearing of

▼ *While surveying Highland roads in the 1720s, Edward Burt recorded a very varied array of tartan outfits.*

the "tartan plaid, philibeg [kilt], purse and other appendages" from Colonel John Small. Shortly afterwards, the prince appeared at a fashionable London masquerade wearing a kilt. At this stage it is quite evident that he regarded Highland attire as a form of fancy dress.

◄ *George IV relished the imposing, theatrical air Highland dress gave him, as in this portrait by David Wilkie.*

GEORGE IV'S STATE OUTFIT

The official visit to Scotland in 1822 provided George with a genuine pretext for wearing tartan on a state occasion, and he seized the opportunity eagerly. His outfit for the reception at Holyrood, procured from George Hunter & Company at exorbitant cost, was made with the finest materials, which included 56m/61yd of satin, 28m/31yd of velvet and almost 18m/20yd of cashmere. The sporran was made of soft, silk-lined, white goatskin and adorned with clusters of gems; the leather brogues were topped with golden rosettes, surrounded with gold filigree; and the belts were decorated with golden buckles, bearing the figure of St Andrew on a saltaire of garnets. The weapons were particularly costly, and included a broadsword, a pair of pistols and an emerald-hilted dirk encased in a scabbard covered in crimson velvet, but the most expensive item was a gold badge on the king's bonnet, which was set with rubies, pearls, diamonds and emeralds.

Ironically, most commentators did not focus on the opulent finery of the costume, preferring to concentrate instead on the extraordinary flesh-coloured pantaloons that the king chose to wear beneath his kilt. George's intention, undoubtedly, was to conceal his unsightly legs, but some believed that it made a travesty of the entire outfit. There was a precedent, however, for this sartorial concoction. On the stage, actors had taken to wearing flesh-coloured tights beneath their kilts when appearing in Scottish productions, such as *Macbeth* or *Rob Roy*. Unconsciously the king was emphasizing the theatricality of Highland dress.

▶ *Alasdair Ranaldson MacDonell of Glengarry was a passionate advocate of Highland dress, as this striking portrait by Raeburn confirms.*

FULL HIGHLAND DRESS

The extravagance of George's costume for his Scottish visit was without parallel in the history of Highland dress, but it did typify a general trend. Among the Highland worthies who attended the royal visit there was a strong competitive element, as each tried to ensure that they created a more striking impression than their rivals in other clans. In many cases, this had less to do with the quality of the materials used than with the quantity of the accessories. For the first time, efforts were made to compile a complete inventory of the items that ought to be included in full Highland dress. The results were a very far cry from the kind of outfit originally worn by penniless Highlanders.

The most exhaustive list of clothes and accessories was provided by Alasdair Ranaldson MacDonell of Glengarry. In common with many of the Highland chiefs, MacDonell commissioned a portrait to show off his tartan finery and, in this, he displayed many of the items specified in his list. He may have intended the painting as the embodiment of an old tradition, but the effect was undermined by two main features. First, the outfit was elaborately tailored, unlike the early forms of Highland attire, which had become popular precisely because their manufacture was so simple. Second, the profusion of guns, swords and knives underlines the fact that MacDonell and many of his contemporaries chose to be portrayed as Highland warriors, even though this bore very little relation to their actual lifestyle. Instead, they were participating in a colourful form of role-playing, inspired by the romantic image that was now evoked by the Jacobites of old.

MACDONELL'S INVENTORY

A Belted Plaid and waist Belt

A Tartan Jacket with True Highlander Buttons and Shoulder Buckles

A Scarlet Vest with True Highlander Buttons

A Cocked Bonnet with Clan Badge and Cockade

A Purse and Belt

A Pair of Highland Garters

A Pair of Hose

A Pair of Highland Brogues

A Gun (or Fusee) with a sling

A Broad Sword and Shoulder Belt

A Target and Slinging Belt

A Brace of Highland Pistols and Belt

A "Chore Dubh" or Hose Knife [*skean dhu*]

A Powder Horn with Chain and Cord

A short Pouch and cross shoulder Belt

THE TARTAN CRAZE

The growing passion for tartan in the 19th century resulted in the creation of a host of societies and clubs devoted to the study and preservation of ancient Scottish culture. The Highland Society of London had already set the benchmark for the other organizations that now sprang up.

THE CELTIC SOCIETY

Originally devised by William Mackenzie of Gruinard, a captain of the Inverness Militia, this Edinburgh-based group was not limited exclusively to Highlanders and was less aristocratic in its composition than some of the other societies. Instead, there was a strong showing from the

▲ *The inaugural meeting of the Society of True Highlanders was held by the ruins of Inverlochy Castle.*

▼ *Traditional music was important to the Highland societies: John Mackenzie was piper to the True Highlanders.*

mercantile class, along with a number of lawyers, doctors and bankers. Sir Walter Scott became the Celtic Society's president and, through his influence, it played a major part in the ceremonial aspects of King George's 1822 visit to Scotland.

Its mixed membership attracted criticism from some quarters, however. Alasdair Ranaldson MacDonell, for example, wrote a stinging letter on the subject to the *Edinburgh Observer*: "I dined one day with them...and I never saw so much tartan before in my life, with so little Highland material...There may be some very good and respectable men amongst them, but their general appearance is assumed and fictitious, and they have no right to burlesque the national character or dress of the Highlands..."

To some degree, MacDonell's remarks stemmed from the rivalry that existed between the Celtic Society and his own group – the True Highlanders.

However, it did also reflect a genuine concern among some Highlanders that their traditions were being hijacked by Lowlanders. In a sense their fears were justified. When in 1804 Sir John Sinclair proposed a motion that tartan should be worn at all future meetings of the society, he stressed that there was an urgent need to assert the unique qualities of Scottish culture, before "Scotland becomes completely confounded in England". This underlined the real value of the tartan revival to Lowland Scots. As the latter's economic ties with England grew ever closer there was a danger that the region would be swallowed up by its southern neighbour. Only by adopting the very distinctive culture of the Highlands as its own could it retain its Scottish national identity.

THE TRUE HIGHLANDERS

The Lowlanders' view cut very little ice with the exclusive membership of the Society of True Highlanders. Founded in 1815, its supporters were drawn entirely from "Highlanders of property and birth", and its declared aims were to promote "the Dress, Language, Music, and Characteristics of our Illustrious and Ancient Race in the Highlands and Islands of Scotland". Many of its activities were actually lavish social events, such as the balls held in the grounds of Inverlochy Castle.

ALASDAIR RANALDSON MacDONELL OF GLENGARRY

The driving force behind the Society of True Highlanders was Alasdair Ranaldson MacDonell, 15th Chief of Glengarry. He was a firm advocate of tradition, even if some of his views belonged to another era. Walter Scott

▼ *Hunting became a popular pastime. This picture by Sir Edwin Landseer depicts a deer-stalking expedition in the Highlands.*

called him "a kind of Quixote in our age, having retained... the whole feelings of clanship and chieftainship, elsewhere so long abandoned. He seems to have lived a century too late..."

MacDonell's commitment to the old ways led him to maintain elements of a traditional Highland court, employing a clan bard and often appearing in public with a piper and servants carrying his weapons. He also liked to go out hunting in the manner of his ancestors, dressed in his plaid and sleeping under the stars. In other respects, however, he was all too modern. Stewart of Garth, for example, accused him of hypocrisy, for playing the role of an old-fashioned Highland chief while at the same time removing many of his tenants from their lands in order to make way for sheep. Ironically for a man who was so dedicated to the past, MacDonell's name is associated with one of the

◄ *The distinctive Glengarry bonnet, linked to the name of MacDonnell, was adopted by several Scottish regiments.*

more recent items of Highland dress – the Glengarry bonnet, which he may have devised.

HIGHLAND SOCIETIES

The rivalry between the Celtic Society and the True Highlanders gave them a high profile during the revival period, but they were by no means unique. New branches of the Highland Society were established in a number of Scottish cities. One of them was founded in Aberdeen where, in common with their London counterparts, members were expected to appear in their clan tartan at every meeting. The society's principal aim was to "promote the general use of the ancient Highland dress," but it also lent support to Gaelic schools, studied the "relics" of Celtic literature, and provided relief for poor Highlanders.

SOCIAL CLUBS

The revival of tartan was also linked with a variety of local social clubs, such as the Highland Mountain Club of Lochgoilhead, formed in 1815. The club espoused the lofty desire to "adopt the dress, cultivate the language, and perpetuate the manners and refined sentiments of our remote ancestors". In practice, this entailed a combination of mountaineering, drinking and musketry, with the members attired in Highland dress. A typical outing would consist of a bracing climb up a local peak, where various songs and toasts were made in Gaelic, each of which was followed by a celebratory burst of gunfire. After this, the members would return downhill "to the reverberating sounds of bagpipes and musquetry".

EARLY HISTORICAL RESEARCH

The numerous Highland organizations that sprang up during the revival period in the 19th century achieved very mixed results. Some were genuinely distinguished bodies that did much to preserve and promote the cause of Highland culture, while others effectively reduced the function of tartan to the level of fancy dress. Outside the clubs and societies, there were also an increasing number of individuals who added their own contributions to the study of the subject.

PRESERVING TRADITIONAL TARTANS

The initiative taken by the Highland Society of London in instituting its tartan survey in 1815 was invaluable, even if the results were not widely publicized. The chief aims of the survey had been to record the old patterns, to prevent them being lost, and to encourage some degree of consistency in the use of tartan. At the time, this was still the exception rather than the rule. When,

TRADITIONAL GARB

In the Highland dress section of *The Scottish Gael*, published in 1831, James Logan was keen to refute the idea that tartan was a comparatively recent development. "It will be proved that this primitive costume, so well suited to the warrior, so well adapted for the avocations of the hunter and shepherd," he wrote, "has not only been the invariable dress of the Highlanders from time immemorial, but is to be derived from the most remote antiquity... Their country and pursuits rendering the belted plaid and kilt the most convenient apparel, they were not likely to lay it aside for any other."

for example, Alexander Robertson of Struan wished to discover the traditional sett for his family, he made enquiries among the elders of his clan. Many of them claimed to know the true design, but the descriptions they supplied were quite different from each other. Accordingly, Robertson was forced to make his own choice and, as he felt that the suggested patterns were "all very vulgar and gaudy", he decided to adopt the Atholl tartan instead.

A UNIQUE ARCHIVE

The Highland Society's survey resulted in the creation of a unique archive, and its efforts were supplemented by a number of enthusiastic tartan collectors. The most notable of these was General Sir William Cockburn, who was a member of the society. Between 1810 and 1820, he built up a collection of 56 specimen tartans, which he catalogued and mounted in a large, leather-bound volume.

The samples Cockburn included in his collection are thought to have been woven by the tartan manufacturers Wilson's of Bannockburn. This is of particular interest, since the results can be compared with the thread-counts and colours specified in the company's own pattern book of 1819. Wilson's went out of business in 1924 and none of their original stock has survived. Most of the specimens they made for Cockburn were of "hard" tartan (a densely woven, coarse wool variety that went out of fashion after the mid-19th century) and they were identified with Cockburn's hand-written labels. These are not without controversy. The Cockburn tartan, for example, was later discovered to be a Mackenzie sett, even though Sir William had confirmed the identification himself. The Cockburn Collection is now housed in Glasgow's Mitchell Library.

▲ *James Logan drew this Highland piper from the 42nd Regiment for his book* The Scottish Gael *(1831).*

THE SCOTTISH GAEL

The first book to include a detailed listing of clan tartans appeared in 1831. This was James Logan's seminal study, *The Scottish Gael or Celtic Manners, as Preserved among the Highlanders*. Logan was born in Aberdeen around 1794, the son of a merchant. He studied at Marischal College with the intention of becoming a lawyer, but following an unfortunate accident – he is said to have been struck on the head by a hammer at an athletics competition – he was unable to complete the course. During his recuperation he became fascinated by early Scottish history and archaeology, and his interest led him to devote much of his career to antiquarian research.

For most of the 1820s Logan earned his living writing articles for newspapers and magazines, while also working on his most important book. The research for this was spread across five years, during which time, in his own words, "with staff in hand and knapsack on his shoulders, he wandered leisurely over all of Scotland, from the Mull of Galloway to John O'Groats...carefully examining and sketching its antiquities of every kind."

When compiling his list of tartans, Logan received assistance from both the Highland Society of London and Wilson's of Bannockburn. The former allowed him to consult their archive of certified tartans, while the latter sent him a summary of the "patterns of all the clan and family tartans". This was annotated with a series of useful comments, such as "MacDougall, as we make it" or, regarding the Douglas sett, that they had been selling it for "a considerable time". Logan published a collection of 55 tartans that he believed to be "as correct as the most laborious personal investigations, and the able assistance of some valued friends, could make it".

▲ *An array of clan shields from Robert McIan's seminal two-volume study,* The Clans of the Scottish Highlands.

After completing *The Scottish Gael,* Logan gained the post of secretary of the Highland Society of London, largely through the good offices of his friend Sir John Sinclair. He subsequently became involved in the Gaelic Society of London, channelling his energies into the promotion of the Gaelic language and its literature. His interest in tartan persisted, however, and he later wrote the text for *The Clans of the Scottish Highlands* (1845–47), which contained an attractive series of 74 engravings by the actor and illustrator Robert Ranald McIan. *The Clans* proved to be one of the most popular books on the subject during the Victorian period. Through it, Logan made the acquaintance of Prince Albert, who helped him to gain lodgings in the Charterhouse to offset the genteel poverty of his declining years.

▼ *McIan's lively pictures of clansmen were the finest of the period. Here, the Lord of the Isles delivers judgment.*

▼ *A barefooted Highland warrior, with his plaid folded around his body, wields a traditional Scottish longsword.*

▼ *Another illustration from McIan shows how women wore the arisaid, the female equivalent of the plaid.*

THE TARTAN FORGERIES

At the height of the 19th century tartan craze new patterns were created at an alarming rate, and many were passed off as traditional designs. The Sobieski brothers appeared on the scene at this time, claiming access to ancient manuscripts that would end all disputes about who had a right to wear what.

The brothers' mysterious origins seemed as romantic as one of Sir Walter Scott's plots. John (1795–1872) and Charles (1797–1880) were the sons of Thomas Allen. The latter believed that he was related to the earls of Errol and adopted their family name

▼ *Jan Sobieski, king of Poland, a name with romantic associations in Scotland because of its links with Prince Charles.*

(Hay), while also changing the spelling of Allen to its Scottish form, Allan. John and Charles Hay Allan went much further, intimating that Thomas Allen had been the legitimate son of Bonnie Prince Charlie and his wife, Louisa of Stolberg-Gedern. Officially, no such child had existed, but a story circulated that a boy had been born in secret and was raised away from court, under an assumed identity, lest the Hanoverians should try to murder him. As well as hinting that they were the offspring of this Stuart heir, the Allen brothers adopted the name of a Polish royal dynasty, Sobieski, since Charlie had been related to this family through his mother. When they made their entrée into Scottish society, they were calling themselves John Sobieski Stolberg Stuart, Count d'Albanie, and Charles Sobieski Stuart.

The brothers spent their early years in Europe, where they claimed to have served with Napoleon's army, and lived for a time in London, where they learned some Gaelic. They arrived in Scotland around 1817, and their charm and cultivated manners soon won them friends in the highest circles. Their chief patron was Lord Lovat, who gave them a house on his estates, on a small island in the Beauly river.

ANCIENT MANUSCRIPTS

Once firmly established in Edinburgh, the brothers gradually revealed the existence of three tartan manuscripts in their possession. The oldest dated back to about 1571 and had apparently been preserved in the Scots College in the French town of Douai. They said it had been presented to Bonnie Prince Charlie and had thus been inherited by Thomas Allen. The Cromarty manuscript, so called because it had been acquired from an old Highlander in that region, was dated 1721, while a third text, supposedly found at the

▼ *The Sobieski brothers became the darlings of Scottish society.*

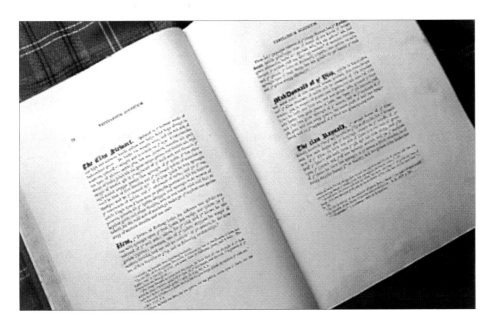

▲ *The* Vestiarium Scoticum *was hugely successful because it suggested that clan tartans had a long pedigree.*

Monastery of St Augustine in Cadiz, in southern Spain, was said to have been written in 1608.

If genuine, these manuscripts would have revolutionized the history of tartan, giving some of the clan setts a pedigree that stretched back to Tudor times. For this very reason, many historians were sceptical, particularly since the Sobieskis seemed so reluctant to let anyone examine the documents. A few privileged individuals were allowed to peruse the Cromarty manuscript, but the other two remained unseen. Sir Walter Scott was even more suspicious when he learned that many of the tartans in the various texts related to the Lowlands, for he had always been convinced that clan tartans had been the sole preserve of the Highlands.

THE *VESTIARIUM SCOTICUM*

The brothers revealed the existence of one of the documents in 1829 to Dick Lauder, a friend of Sir Walter Scott, and, after years of prevaricating, they eventually published its contents in *Vestiarium Scoticum* (1842). This contained colour illustrations of 75 tartans, many of them hitherto unknown. From the outset, the *Vestiarium* proved highly controversial. Nevertheless, when the book was finally published, it won many supporters. Several clans adopted, and indeed are still wearing, patterns that first appeared in its pages. A proper, scientific analysis of the manuscripts has never been possible, since none of them have ever been found, if indeed they ever existed. The only evidence has come from a series of photographs of the Cromarty manuscript, taken around 1895. These suggest that the documents had been artificially aged, and probably only dated from the early 19th century. On the internal evidence of the manuscript, too, there was one key finding. The text included an accurate description of the Gordon regimental tartan, even though it is clear from surviving correspondence that this was chosen much later, in 1793.

Undeterred by the controversy, the Sobieski brothers continued to produce books on Scottish traditions. They included the *Lays of the Deer Forest*, as well as another, less contentious book about tartan, *The Costume of the Clans*. In later years, the Sobieskis moved to Austria, then finally settled in England.

INVENTED SETTS

Serious scholars sometimes despaired at the proliferation of tartans making the rounds. Thomas Dick Lauder complained to his friend Sir Walter Scott: "In these times of rage for tartans…the most uncouth coats of many colours are every day invented, manufactured, christened after particular names and worn as genuine… At present, a woeful want of knowledge in the subject prevails. Some of the clans are at this moment ignorantly disputing for the right to the same tartans, which in fact belong to none of them, but are merely modern inventions for clothing Regimental Highlanders. Hardly does one of the clans now wear its tartan with its legitimate setts."

▶ *An officer of the 92nd Regiment, also known as the Gordon Highlanders.*

QUEEN VICTORIA'S SEAL OF APPROVAL

The gimmickry of George IV's state visit to Scotland kick-started the tartan revival, but did not guarantee its survival. After 1822, the king never again demonstrated the same level of interest in his northern kingdom. Instead, it was his niece, Queen Victoria, who developed a genuine fondness for the Highlands and did much to ensure the lasting popularity of tartan.

Victoria and her husband Prince Albert paid their first visit to the area in 1842, two years after they were married. They were received with due pomp and pageantry, but without the element of fancy dress that had attended George's trip. At Dunkeld, they were greeted by a spectacular gathering of the Atholl clans. Shortly afterwards, they were given an even grander reception at Taymouth Castle, which the queen recorded enthusiastically in her journal: "The *coup d'oeil* was

▲ *Queen Victoria described Balmoral, built in the Scottish baronial style, as "this dear Paradise".*

COMMERCIAL HIGHLANDISM

Queen Victoria's growing fondness for spending time in the far north of Britain coincided with rapid improvements in communications. New railway lines and shipping routes, together with the blossoming of the tourist industry, brought visitors flocking to Scotland. This in turn generated a demand for suitable souvenirs and memorabilia. Suddenly, tartan designs were no longer confined to woven materials, but could be found on every imaginable form of knick-knack – from tea caddies and spectacle cases to cheap jewellery and plates. "Highlandism" had found a powerful commercial outlet: one that has continued to thrive to the present day.

indescribable. There were a number of Lord Breadalbane's Highlanders, all in the Campbell tartan, drawn up in front of the house, with Lord Breadalbane himself in a Highland dress at their head…a number of pipers playing, and a company of the 92nd Highlanders, also in kilts. The firing of the guns, the cheering of the great crowd, the picturesqueness of the country… altogether formed one of the finest scenes imaginable. It seemed as if a great chieftain in olden feudal times was receiving his sovereign. It was princely and romantic."

The trip was such a success that the royal couple were eager to return and, in 1844, they stayed for several weeks at Blair Castle. Three years later, they toured the Hebrides in the royal yacht and enjoyed an extended break at Ardverikie by Loch Laggan.

BALMORAL

In 1848, Victoria and Albert leased Balmoral for the first time, swiftly realizing that this was the ideal place for them. Four years later, they bought the

estate and set about remodelling it to suit their own needs. A local architect, William Smith of Aberdeen, rebuilt part of the structure in the Scottish baronial style. The interior was very largely designed by Prince Albert and included a series of "cheerful and un-palace-like rooms" that conjured up the atmosphere of a cosy but elegant hunting lodge, enlivened with chintzes and tartans. Once the improvements were in place, it became a favourite retreat for the couple. For both Victoria and Albert, and indeed for many of their successors, Balmoral represented a genuine sanctuary, where they could escape from the rigours and formality of court life. The relaxing atmosphere was confirmed by an outside observer, Charles Greville, who noted of the royal family, "They live there without any state whatever: they live not merely like private gentlefolks, but like very small gentlefolks…"

BALMORAL TARTANS

Prince Albert's interior design for Balmoral included many tartans. The Royal Stewart and Hunting Stewart patterns were used for the carpets, while the curtains and upholstery mainly featured the Dress Stewart sett. In addition, two new tartans were created to add variety to the decor. The queen herself was fond of the design called Victoria, a subtle variant of Royal Stewart, while Prince Albert devised an entirely new sett for the project. Known as Balmoral, this tartan is still popular, although its use is restricted solely to members of the royal family.

▼ *The Balmoral tartan, devised by Albert for use at the castle.*

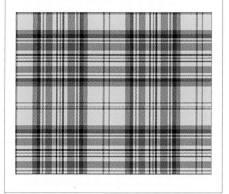

Victoria was the first reigning monarch for several centuries to choose to spend a significant amount of time in Scotland. In doing so, she tacitly gave the royal seal of approval to an entire range of Highland activities. It was no longer unusual for the British public to hear or read of the queen being attended by pipers, or the royal children playing in kilts, or Prince Albert watching the Highland games. Victoria's links with the Highlands

▼ *This depiction of Queen Victoria's personal sitting room at Balmoral appeared in an early edition of her Highland journals.*

▲ *Returning from the hunt at night, Prince Albert proudly displays to Victoria the game that has been killed.*

remained strong, even after Albert's premature death in 1861. She went into a protracted period of mourning, virtually retiring from public life, and her eventual recovery owed much to the loyalty and support of her Highland servant, John Brown. Their friendship stirred up gossip in some quarters of the press, as rumours circulated that they were having an affair. A few mischief-makers even suggested that they had married in secret, dubbing the queen "Mrs Brown".

On a less contentious level, Victoria also maintained the high profile of the Highlands through two influential publications. In 1868, a carefully edited version of her journal, entitled *Leaves from the Journal of Our Life in the Highlands*, appeared in print and became an instant bestseller. This was followed two years later by *The Highlanders of Scotland*, the preparation of which Victoria supervised closely. She commissioned for it a lavish set of illustrations from the watercolourist Kenneth MacLeay. These consisted of a series of portraits of individual Highlanders in full costume, which must rank among the very finest images of tartan ever produced.

TARTAN IN ART

Initially, the portrayal of tartan in the visual arts was largely confined to costume prints and commissioned portraits. With both of these, there was a tendency to emphasize the exotic nature of Highland dress, as a form of attire entirely distinct from that of other European nations. Accordingly, some artists were encouraged to exaggerate the complexity of the garb, by combining it with a gaudy jacket or hat, or by adding a profusion of accessories. There is some irony in this, given that the plaid owed its longevity to the simplicity of its design and to the fact that even a modest crofter could afford it. Despite this, the extravagance of some portraits was noticeable from an early stage. The 17th-century outfit depicted in John Michael Wright's *Lord Mungo Murray*, for example, was spectacular, if hardly convincing as typical hunting attire.

▼ *Raeburn's portrait of the MacNab exudes pride and resilience, typifying the Romantic view of the Highlander.*

TARTAN IN PORTRAITS

The vogue for tartan portraits reached a peak in the 18th and early 19th centuries. Some were commissioned as statements of national or political identity, although in many cases patrons and artists were simply seduced by the glamour of the costume. This was particularly true of the Neoclassical painters who flourished in the 18th century. They were interested in recapturing the spirit and grandeur of the

▲ *Millais's* The Order of Release *was a trial for the artist, as the child and the dog proved restless models.*

ancient world in their pictures, and Highland dress proved eminently suitable for this. Both the kilt and the belted plaid bore a passing resemblance to a toga, while the sweep of tartan material over the shoulder carried echoes of classical drapery. This enabled artists to endow Highland figures with the nobility of an ancient warrior or the dignity of a classical philosopher. Pompeo Batoni's portrait of William Gordon is an example of the former, while Allan Ramsay's elegant depiction of the 22nd chief of the MacLeods typifies the latter.

ROMANTICISM

Highland subjects were equally popular with Romantic portraitists, who were attracted by the Celtic origins of the costume, its associations with a rebellious and independent people, and the tragic overtones of its history. The pictures were often composed in a very theatrical manner, with a low viewpoint to heighten the sense of drama and a spectacular background. Typical of this was Henry Raeburn's vivid portrait, *The MacNab*, which showed a stern-faced old man kitted out in the guise of a young warrior and posing on a bleak mountain-top, while stormclouds gathered in the distance. Evidently, portraits of this kind were designed to create a strong, emotional impact. In part, this was due to the fact that they were normally sent to London to be exhibited at the Royal Academy – a factor that the artist would have taken into account when designing his composition.

SENTIMENTAL SCENES

The taste for extravagant Highland portraits began to wane after 1822, surfeited perhaps by the pageantry of George IV's visit. Tartan featured increasingly in other types of painting, however, notably in the narrative and sentimental scenes so beloved by the Victorians. The most celebrated was John Millais's *The Order of Release*, which managed to combine a dog, a child and a fallen woman in a single composition. The picture shows a Highland soldier gaining his freedom, presumably after Culloden. He is greeted by his family but, overcome with emotion, fails to notice the

solemn expression of his wife. This, coupled with the trampled blooms at her feet, suggests that she has paid for his liberty with her virtue.

With typical thoroughness, Millais researched the tartans in Robert Ranald McIan's *Clans of the Scottish Highlands*, opting for the Gordon and Drummond setts. The model for the wife was Effie Ruskin, a Scot, and she approved of the theme, describing it as "quite Jacobite and after my own heart". The painting was exhibited at the Royal Academy in 1853, where it met with huge acclaim. One newspaper reported that the artist had attracted "a larger crowd of admirers in his little corner...than all the Academicians put together," and eventually the organizers had to station a policeman beside the painting to chivvy the spectators along.

Jacobite themes proved a popular subject for many Victorian painters. John Pettie, for example, earned considerable praise for *Disbanded*, which showed a Jacobite soldier heading home, with a sack full of Hanoverian loot slung over his shoulder. There was

also a market for more contemporary illustrations of the Highland way of life. These touched on some very thorny issues, such as emigration and the clearances, though the artists rarely adopted a critical stance and most seemed content to focus on the picturesque qualities of their chosen scene.

Several painters depicted the shooting parties that were becoming commonplace in the Highlands, on land that had formerly been occupied by crofters. Typical examples include Carl Haag's *Morning in the Highlands* and Richard Ansdell's *A Shooting Party in the Highlands*. Rosa Bonheur's charming animal studies hinted at changes in the farming world. In *Changing Pastures*, she painted a boat, crammed full of sheep, being rowed across a loch. The scene appears faintly whimsical until one remembers that the sheep, like the shooting parties, had displaced many Highland families.

▼ *Rosa Bonheur's painting has poignant overtones, as the rise of sheep-farming led to many evictions.*

MASS EMIGRATION

By the middle years of Queen Victoria's reign, tartan and the ancient culture of the Highlands were firmly established as symbols of Scotland's national identity. There was a cruel irony about this, given that the Highlands themselves were in crisis. As a succession of economic disasters hit home, many Scots were forced to emigrate, turning the romantic image of Highlandism into a hollow myth.

Owing to the precarious nature of Highland agrarian economy, emigration had always been a fact of life, but the situation deteriorated considerably in the 19th century. The clearances had begun in the closing years of the previous century, as entire townships were evicted to make way for huge sheep farms. On the Sutherland estates alone, more than 7,000 people were moved out between 1807 and 1821.

▼ *Relatives on the quayside wave goodbye, as an emigrant ship is towed out of a Scottish harbour to begin its journey to Sydney.*

ECONOMIC PROBLEMS
The initial phase of the clearances had peaked by 1820, but the Highlands were soon affected by other problems. After the end of the Napoleonic wars, the region lost some of its export markets and faced stiffer competition from cheap imports. The herring industry went into a steep decline and the processing of kelp (a type of seaweed) for use in the glass and soap industries was no longer profitable. On top of this, there was an influx of demobilized and unemployed soldiers from the Highland regiments.

These economic woes placed added pressure on Highland landowners, many of whose estates were already mortgaged to the hilt. As a result, most were forced to sell up or place their lands in trust. It has been estimated that in the first half of the 19th century, more than two-thirds of Highland properties changed hands. Many of the new owners were Lowlanders or Englishmen, who had few inhibitions about taking the drastic measures that were deemed necessary in order to restore the viability of the large estates. Sheep farming remained the most popular choice, but it was not the only option. Some areas were turned into sporting playgrounds for the rich, with facilities for hunting, shooting and fishing. In 1835, this led a correspondent from the *Inverness Courier* to comment, "Even unconquerable barrenness is now turned to good account. At the present moment, we believe, many Highland proprietors derive a greater revenue from their moors alone, for grouse shooting, than their whole rental amounted to sixty years since."

THE POTATO FAMINE
For those who had survived the worst of the economic difficulties, a new horror awaited. In 1846, the potato crops failed, destroyed by the *Phytophthora infestans* fungus, which had already caused devastation in many parts of Europe. The Hebrides and the western mainland were the worst affected areas of Scotland, but nowhere was immune to the problem. Throughout the Highlands, every community became all too familiar with the sickly stench of rotting potatoes.

The effects were catastrophic. A standard cereal crop might fail one year and recover the next, but the potato blight lingered for over a decade. This was particularly serious given that the poorest districts relied heavily on the potato for their survival.

Once the scale of the problem became apparent, efforts were made to provide famine relief. Committees were set up in Glasgow and Edinburgh to raise money for the purchase of oatmeal, and by 1847 their work was co-ordinated by the Central Board of Management for Highland Relief. In addition to supplying food, some local authorities initiated new construction

projects in order to provide work for the destitute. Money and food also came in from Scottish expatriates in Canada and the United States, as well as from charitable appeals throughout Britain. Even some of the least prosperous members of society were keen to contribute – servants at Cramond House, the inmates of the asylum at Dumfries and workers at Dalkeith Colliery all managed to donate hard-earned cash.

THE LONG-TERM SOLUTION

In spite of these efforts, it was clear that emigration offered the only genuine long-term solution to the problem, and this occurred on a massive scale. In the immediate aftermath of the famine, the islands of Barra and Jura lost a third of their population, for example, and this type of figure was by no means exceptional. Many of those who left took advantage of assisted emigration

schemes run by such organizations as the Highlands and Islands Emigration Society, or by the government's Colonial Land and Emigration Department. These were ostensibly concerned with helping the destitute to leave the country, although it became increasingly clear that they had a second agenda – namely, to provide able-bodied labour for the colonies. In their own words, they preferred to help those who were "a burden to the British community in the Mother Country" to become "a support to it when transferred to the Colonies."

Concerns about emigration were mirrored in the work of many Scottish artists, although, in true Victorian fashion, they were generally interested in the pathos rather than the politics of the situation. This was particularly evident in the paintings of Thomas Faed. He produced touching portrayals of homesick emigrants yearning for their

▲ *Thomas Faed won plaudits for his touching domestic scenes. Here he depicts a group of Scottish settlers in North America.*

native land, as well as tender scenes of families bidding farewell to their loved ones. His most famous picture in this vein was *The Last of the Clan*, which depicted an aged Highlander, too old to make the journey, watching his children sail away from Scotland forever. When the painting was exhibited at the Royal Academy, Faed added an explanatory note, which might have served equally well as an epitaph for many of the Highland clans: "When the steamer had slowly backed out...we began to feel that our once powerful clan was now represented by a feeble old man and his grand-daughter who, together with some outlying kith and kin, owned not a single blade of grass in the glen that was once all our own."

REGIMENTAL TARTANS

WHEN HIGHLAND DRESS WAS BANNED IN CIVILIAN CIRCLES, IT COULD STILL BE WORN BY THOSE WHO JOINED ONE OF THE SCOTTISH REGIMENTS WITHIN THE BRITISH ARMY. THROUGH THEIR EXPLOITS AROUND THE WORLD, THE REPUTATION OF TARTAN REACHED NEW HEIGHTS.

EARLY MILITARY TARTANS

It has been suggested that tartan owes its survival to the Scots' reputation as soldiers. For, when the Hanoverian government decided to outlaw Highland dress in 1746, it allowed certain exceptions. The most important of these concerned a number of Scottish regiments, which were given permission to retain their traditional attire.

The reasoning behind this was simple. The Jacobite rebellions had occurred at a period when the British Empire was expanding at a prodigious rate, and more troops than ever were required to protect national interests. By encouraging Highlanders to enlist, the authorities meant to meet this need while also ensuring that some of their most troublesome subjects were removed from their homeland.

SCOTTISH MERCENARIES
The Scots had long been renowned for their military prowess, a reputation dating back to early periods of emigration, when Highlanders often hired themselves out as mercenaries. The links with France were particularly strong, and the Scots formed the core of two elite corps: *Les Gardes du Corps Ecossaises* (the Scottish Guard of Archers), who served as bodyguards to

▲ *The district tartan from Romsdal, Norway, where Scots landed in 1612.*

▼ *The Gudbrandsdalen is based on a jacket worn by a fallen Scottish soldier.*

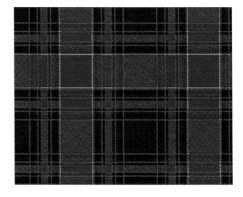

the French king, and *Les Gens d'Armes Ecossaises* (Scottish Men-At-Arms).

Not all exploits of the Highlanders were as distinguished as this. Two modern tartans – Gudbrandsdalen and Romsdal – commemorate a military disaster from 1612. Colonel George Sinclair raised a contingent of his clansmen in Caithness, and led them into action as mercenaries in Sweden. Sinclair landed his men at Romsdal, on the coast of Norway, and took them through the narrow pass of Gudbrandsdal. Here, the clansmen were ambushed by local peasants, who hurled down rocks from the heights, bringing their campaign to a premature end. The Gudbrandsdalen tartan is said

Previous pages: Eilean Donan Castle.

SOLDIERS IN TARTAN
While they were stationed at Stettin (now Szczecin, in Poland), the colourful dress of Mackay's Regiment attracted the attention of an anonymous local artist, who produced a woodcut of the costumes. Although the men were described as Irish, there is little doubt that this represents the earliest image of Scottish soldiers wearing tartan. Three of the figures are shown in plaids, while the fourth is wearing baggy breeches and matching hose. All the men have bonnets. The depictions of the plaids illustrate the different ways that the garment could be worn: one soldier wears it belted at the waist; the second has it draped around him, like a cloak or blanket; while the third wears it looped over his right shoulder.

▼ *Soldiers from Mackay's Regiment in Stettin in 1631.*

▲ Gustavus Adolphus of Sweden employed Scots soldiers in his lengthy wars against the Catholic powers.

▶ A soldier of Mackay's Regiment, which was dubbed the "right hand" of Gustavus Adolphus.

to be based on a jacket worn by one of the fallen men.

Many other Scots travelled to Sweden and Germany to enlist as mercenaries in the Thirty Years' War. Thousands of Highlanders are said to have served under Gustavus Adolphus (r.1611–1632), the so-called Lion of the North, including no fewer than three field marshals, 14 generals, 41 colonels and 20 captains.

MACKAY'S REGIMENT

For the student of tartan the most significant of these may have been Donald, Chief of Mackay, who was created Lord Reay in 1628. Two years prior to this, he obtained permission from Charles I to raise a force of 3000 men to serve in Germany.

Around a third came from his own clan, while the remainder were recruited from other Highland families. This force became known as Mackay's Regiment.

The regiment fought for the Protestant cause, and their numerous feats were publicized in Robert Monro's personal chronicle of the war, published in 1637. The author heaped fulsome praise upon the soldiers' deeds, declaring, "The memory thereof shall never be forgotten, but shall live in spite of time."

THE ROYAL COMPANY OF ARCHERS

Some military bodies adopted tartan in an official capacity long before the Disarming Act of 1746 was put in place. Ironically, the earliest example relates to a

▲ The charter of the Royal Company of Archers provided for public butts to be set up for annual competitions.

Lowland force, rather than a Highland one. For in 1713, the Royal Company of Archers, the Queen's Bodyguard in Scotland, adopted a bright red sett as their new uniform. There has been speculation that tartan was chosen as a form of protest against the Act of Union, but this seems highly unlikely as contemporaneous medals suggest that most archers of the period wore tartan. More tellingly still, the royal family commissioned a portrait of the young Prince George wearing the outfit in question. This rare image of a Hanoverian dressed in tartan underlines the fact that, in the early part of the 18th century at least, the influence of Highland costume did not seem remotely threatening.

The Royal Company of Archers was not a standard regiment. Instead it was more akin to the civic militia of Holland, drawing its membership from prominent local citizens and mainly performing ceremonial duties. The Archers later changed their colours to a predominantly green sett, which can be seen in the portraits of Sir James Pringle and Dr Nathaniel Spens, commissioned in 1791 from David Martin and Henry Raeburn respectively.

THE BLACK WATCH

In 1667, Charles II authorized the 2nd Earl of Atholl to raise an independent company of Highlanders to keep a "watch upon the braes [upland areas]", to counter widespread lawlessness in the area. The company proved a considerable success as a form of police force and by the end of the century several others, generally known as the Watch, had been established. According to a contemporary observer, each was composed of "Highlanders cloathed in their ancient, proper, Caledonian Dress and armed all with Broad Swords, Targets [shields], Guns, Side-pistols and Durks, alias Daggers".

For all its merits, the Watch did nothing to prevent the Jacobite rebellion of 1715 and, indeed, some of their men took part in it. As a result, it was disbanded two years later, and replaced with garrisons of English or Lowland troops. But the usefulness of the independent companies was not forgotten, and when Major-General Wade was entrusted with the task of pacifying the Highlands, he revived the idea. In 1725, six independent companies were established. Three were placed under the command of Campbell chiefs, while the remainder were led by Lord Lovat, Colonel Grant of Ballindalloch and George Munro of Culcairn.

THE GOVERNMENT TARTAN
The Black Watch tartan became instantly recognizable as the badge of the Highland companies and, for most of the 18th century, it was commonly

▶ *Black Watch uniforms through the ages (top to bottom, left to right): officer, piper and sergeant (1739); private (1742); officer (1770); piper (1840); private and officer at the battle of Alexandria (1801); corporal, drummer and private (1845); officer in full dress (1830).*

described as "the Government tartan". It also became the basis for several other regimental tartans, which were usually distinguished from the original design by the addition of one or more coloured over-stripes. In some cases, the pattern was retained without alteration, which could have unforeseen benefits.

The "new" Sutherland tartan, for example, which was worn by the Argyll and Sutherland Highlanders, was identical to the Black Watch design. When the unprecedented demand for tartan prior to George IV's 1822 visit to Scotland caused it to be in very short supply, the Sutherland commander managed to

▶ *Military uniforms were simplified in the 19th century. Some regiments adopted shakos (caps) in place of bearskins, or trews instead of plaids.*

persuade Wilson's of Bannockburn to send them a batch of plaids that had actually been promised to a Black Watch garrison in Ireland.

REGIMENTAL STATUS

Meanwhile, the Black Watch performed its duties well and four new companies were added in 1739, bringing it up to full regiment strength. This was placed under the command of the Earl of Crawford and, following a muster at Aberfeldy in 1740, it was numbered the 43rd Regiment.

As long as they were stationed in the Highlands, the soldiers of the new regiment acquitted themselves well. However, a lingering mistrust, both on the part of the clansmen and the government, surfaced during the 1740s, when Britain was becoming increasingly embroiled in the War of the Austrian Succession and required more troops for service in Europe. The war coincided with growing fears of another Jacobite uprising, so the authorities in London deemed it prudent to remove the Highlanders from their homeland, lest they join the cause. Accordingly, in 1743, the order was given for the Black Watch to march south.

A SHORT-LIVED MUTINY

This caused consternation among the Gaelic-speaking Highlanders, many of whom had enlisted in the firm belief that they were to be used as peace-keepers in Scotland. However, they were given assurances that the only reason for the journey was to take part in a review, staged for the benefit of the king, and that they would afterwards be allowed to return to the Highlands.

Having marched to London, the Black Watch discovered that the king was absent and their review was to be supervised by Major-General Wade. Their suspicions immediately revived amid rumours that they were about to be sent to the West Indies. By reputa-

tion, this was one of the most unwelcome postings, partly because of its ignominious association with transportation and partly because of its fever-ridden conditions. The resulting short-lived mutiny, during which many of the soldiers tried to march back to Scotland, was swiftly suppressed and three of the ringleaders were executed.

▼ *As one of the ringleaders of a mutiny of the Black Watch in 1743, Corporal Samuel Macpherson was executed in the Tower of London.*

BLACK WATCH TARTAN

When six new companies were formed in 1725, Wade was anxious to impose a degree of uniformity on his forces, so he gave orders for "the plaid of each Company to be as near as they can to the same Sort and Colour". The resulting pattern, dominated by blues and greens, had the subdued tones of a hunting sett. From an early stage it earned the soldiers the nickname Am Freiceadan Dubh (the Black Watch). This referred not only to the dark colouring of the tartan, but also to the fact that one of the force's principal functions was to suppress cattle theft, known as the "black trade".

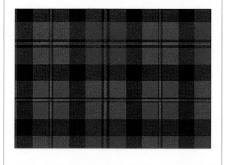

THE HIGHLAND REGIMENTS

After the Jacobite defeat at Culloden in 1746, a series of new Highland regiments was rapidly formed. As soldiers were exempt from the ban on wearing tartan it is tempting to believe that many recruits enlisted as a means of preserving a vestige of their traditional way of life, but this may be too romantic a view. In reality, the Highland economy had already been in decline prior to the 1745 rebellion, and the ruling Hanoverians' punitive measures after the uprising simply aggravated this further. As a result, many ordinary clansmen simply faced a bleak choice between joining the army or starving.

FRASER'S HIGHLANDERS

In fact, the main incentives were directed at the nobility. For those whose lands had been forfeited after the uprising, or who feared the threat of future reprisals, the offer of raising

THE GORDON TARTAN

In 1793, William Forsythe of Huntly, acting as an agent of Wilson's of Bannockburn, wrote to the Duke of Gordon regarding the choice of regimental tartan, enclosing three separate tartan samples. These featured different versions of the Black Watch pattern, showing how it would look with one, two or three yellow over-stripes. "When the plaids are worn, the yellow stripes will be square and regular," Forsythe assured his client. "I imagine the yellow stripes will appear very lively." In the end, the Duke selected the single-stripe design for the Gordon Highlanders, while the Gordon-Cummings adopted two stripes and the Gordons of Esslemont chose the remaining option.

a regiment provided a convenient way to curry official favour. The Frasers of Lovat epitomized this approach. Simon Fraser, 11th Lord Lovat, had been a prominent Jacobite and was executed in 1747. His son had also taken part in the rebellion, but he was pardoned and, in 1757, was given permission to raise a regiment (the 78th or Fraser's Highlanders). This was a difficult task, given that the family estates had been forfeited, but the loyalty of the clan soon brought him sufficient recruits. Fraser's Highlanders served with distinction both in Canada and, as the

▲ *A soldier from the 79th Cameron Highlanders, pictured in 1853.*

71st Regiment, in the United States. Arguably their finest hour came in 1759, when they played a major part in Wolfe's victory at Quebec. At first light, they had the unenviable task of clambering up a precipitous cliff, disposing of a French battery at the summit, and then guarding the cliff path, while their comrades made their ascent. Feats such as these eventually enabled Fraser to buy back the forfeited Lovat estates.

Many Highlanders took part in the American War of Independence, which began with this confrontation at Lexington in 1775.

LAND GRANTS IN THE NEW WORLD

Many of the newly formed Highland regiments followed a similar path and went to fight in the Americas. Between 1756 and 1763, several took part in the Seven Years' War, in which Britain competed with France for control of the New World. Prominent among these were Montgomery's Highlanders (the 77th Regiment), which was composed of volunteers from a number of the Jacobite clans, including the Camerons, the MacLeans, the Frasers and the MacDonalds.

Once peace had been concluded through the Treaty of Paris, most of the forces were disbanded. Some were brought back to Scotland, while others were given the option of receiving a grant of land in proportion to their rank and making a new home for themselves where they had been fighting. In the case of Fraser's Highlanders, more than 300 of the men decided to settle in Canada, forming a strong clan presence that remains to this day.

THE WAR OF AMERICAN INDEPENDENCE

The recruiting campaigns started all over again just a few years later, when troops were needed by the government to fight in the War of Independence (1775–81). On this occasion, the new regiments included the Fraser Highlanders (now the 71st Regiment), the Argyll Highlanders, and the Highland Light Infantry (MacLeod's Highlanders). Remarkably, the government also persuaded many of those clansmen who had already settled in America to take up arms in their cause. Most of these joined the 84th Royal Highland Emigrant Regiment, which was based in Canada. Included in their number was Allan MacDonald of Kingsburgh, the husband of Flora MacDonald. He was captured at the battle of Moore's Creek and held prisoner for over a year. Once peace had been agreed the regiment was disbanded and Allan received a grant of 700 acres of land in Nova Scotia.

REGIMENTAL TARTANS

Most of the Highland regiments adopted a tartan that was closely based on the Black Watch sett, although individual commanders had a say in the matter. In the case of the Gordon tartan, for example, the surviving correspondence has shed an interesting light on the way the system worked.

The chief exception was the 79th Cameron Highlanders (The Queen's Own Cameron Highlanders). Raised in 1793, this was one of the last regiments to be recruited through family influence. The driving force was Alan Cameron of Erracht, who had served in America with the 84th Royal Highland Emigrant Regiment and had been a prisoner-of-war for two years.

Upon Alan Cameron's return to Scotland, he obtained permission to raise a regiment, together with Ranald MacDonell of Keppoch. The two men wanted a regimental sett that combined elements from both their clan tartans, but this proved difficult, since both had red grounds, which did not suit the scarlet of the military doublet. Ultimately, the solution was found by Lady Erracht, Alan's mother, who created a pattern that merged details of the Cameron sett with those of one of the darker tartans belonging to the Clan Donald.

These sergeants from the 78th Highlanders, also known as the Ross-shire Buffs, were photographed during their service in Canada.

THE FENCIBLE REGIMENTS

In addition to the regiments that served Britain's interests overseas, the country required a domestic military force to protect its own shores. This need was fulfilled by the various fencible regiments. The term originated as a diminutive of "defensible", referring to those men who were deemed suitable for defensive duties, and dated from the 16th century, when it was applied to part-timers fit only for militia duties. During the 18th century, and particularly in the Napoleonic era when the threat of invasion was very real, the authorities saw the advantage of using a more professional, full-time force.

For reasons of economy, the government wanted the services of the

▼ *A contemporary engraving of 1743 illustrates different types of highland uniform and dress.*

fencibles for fairly brief periods only. The earliest examples, the Argyll and the Sutherland Fencibles, were in existence for a mere four years (1759–63). The next three companies lasted just one year longer (1778–83). When Henry Dundas, as Home Secretary, decided to revive the policy at the outbreak of war in 1793, the fencible system mushroomed. Within six years more than 20 regiments had been founded, although most were disbanded by 1802.

TERMS OF CONTRACT

In theory at least, most of the Highland troops recruited for the fencible regiments were meant to serve within the nation's frontiers. More specifically, the soldiers were not to be garrisoned outside Scotland "except in the event of a landing by the enemy upon the coast of England". As with the Black Watch, however, the government wasted no time in breaking its promises when deemed expedient. Accordingly, several regiments were stationed in southern England or sent to deal with a rebellion in Ireland. A few were posted further afield. The Argylls, for example, were despatched to Gibraltar.

These contract changes caused discontent and, in the most extreme cases, outright mutiny. The worst example occurred in 1804, when attempts were being made to raise a regiment of Canadian Fencibles, that is, a regiment of Highlanders prepared to serve in Canada. Initial recruiting had gone well, apparently because the volunteers had been chosen from one of the clearance areas. It soon transpired, however, that the recruiters had overstepped the mark. As the investigating officer later reported: "The men of this corps were ordered to assemble in Glasgow, where it was discovered that the most scandalous deceptions had been practised upon them and that terms had been promised that Government would not, and could not, sanction. The persons who had deceived these poor men... obtained a great number of recruits without any, or for a very small bounty." When the truth was revealed to the recruits, there was uproar and the entire project had to be abandoned.

THE GLENGARRY FENCIBLES

By contrast, the experience of the Glengarry Fencibles was far more encouraging. This regiment was raised from a community of Catholic emigrants who had been shipwrecked off the Scottish coast, not far from Glasgow. Destitute and unable to continue their journey, their future looked bleak until a local priest, Father MacDonell, came up with a solution. He persuaded the men to enlist as

▶ *Sir John Sinclair of Ulbster,*
portrayed here by Henry Raeburn,
designed the distinctive uniform worn
by his own fencible regiment.

soldiers, under his kinsman Alexander MacDonell, Chief of Glengarry. As the Glengarry Fencibles the troops remained in service for eight years (1794–1802), stationed on the islands of Jersey and Guernsey.

When the regiment was disbanded, along with the other fencibles, Father MacDonell petitioned for assistance in helping the men and their families emigrate to Canada. This was eventually granted and 200 acres of land in Ontario were allotted to each of the former soldiers. They named their new settlement Glengarry County and revived the Glengarry Fencibles when trouble erupted during the American War of 1812, which was fought between Britain and the USA along the Canadian border.

SIR JOHN SINCLAIR OF ULBSTER

The fencible regiments adopted a variety of costumes. The most eye-catching, perhaps, belonged to the Rothesay and Caithness Fencibles, which had been raised in 1794. Their colonel was the flamboyant Sir John Sinclair of Ulbster, who had recruited the regiment at the request of the Prime Minister, William Pitt.

Sinclair had wide-ranging interests: he was a maverick politician, an "improving" agriculturalist, the founder of the British Wool Society, and a tireless pamphleteer who produced more than 300 tracts, including several on the origins of Highland dress. This led him to design the uniform for his own regiment, along with an elaborate dress version for the officers. Sinclair was delighted with the results and commissioned a portrait from Henry Raeburn, which showed him wearing the outfit. Others were less impressed,

however, and a friend remarked: "One day he treated us with a sight of him in the Uniform of his Rothesay and Caithness Regiment, and a more curious figure I never saw. The Coat was the only part of his Dress not perfectly outlandish. Scarlet turned up with yellow, a large silk Plaid, partaking of the Nature of a Spanish Cloak crossed before and was flung over one shoulder. Trousers of the same Silk halfway down the leg and checked Red and White Stockings. He was not quite compleat, as he had not his Scotch bonnet, which would have added a foot or so to his Stature."

REGIMENTAL WEAVERS

Prior to the battle of Culloden in 1746, most tartans were woven either at home or by independent weavers, but the coming of the Highland regiments had a profound effect on both the form and the production of tartan. As the traditional sources were no longer sufficient, specialized firms emerged, which dealt specifically with the army. The need for a standardized military uniform resulted in a consistency of design that had not materialized under the clan system, while the sheer volume of kilts and plaids required by the regiments prompted a change in production methods.

WILSON'S OF BANNOCKBURN

The most influential of the new companies was William Wilson & Sons (commonly referred to as Wilson's), based in Bannockburn, close to the city of Stirling. Wilson founded his firm in about 1770 to service the needs of the growing number of regiments, and his two sons, James and William, later expanded the business. They provided uniforms for the wars in America and for the lengthy Napoleonic campaigns. When peace was finally achieved, Wilson's successfully exploited the new market that was opening up in fashionable circles. In 1822, the year of

▲ The Royal George, Wilson's original mill, is the distant white building in the middle of this view of Bannockburn.

George IV's visit to Scotland, the company installed 40 new looms at their works to meet demand.

For historians, the most crucial legacy of Wilson's operations is their pattern books. Although these date from a comparatively late stage in the firm's history (1819 and 1847), they provide a unique insight into the way that the tartan industry was changing. Notes in the books make it clear that Wilson went to some trouble to acquire early, authentic designs. He employed agents to travel through the Highlands, seeking out the "true" exam-

▼ Wilson tartan was named after Janet Wilson, the wife of the founder.

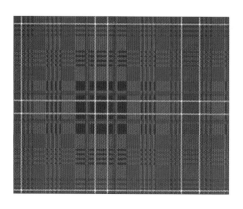

ples that handloom weavers were still producing in small quantities for their local areas. Many clan tartans that are now regarded as traditional were originally identified in this way.

Wilson's longevity also owed much to their forward-looking commercial instincts. During the 19th-century revival period, when tartans were very much in vogue, they created their own designs, advertising the "newest" or "latest" setts for individual clans. Their pattern books also contain scores of unidentified designs, which were intended as "off-the-peg" tartans for customers who wanted to wear a "traditional" family tartan.

FANCY TARTANS

Wilson's seem to have invented the notion of "fancy" tartans for purely decorative purposes. Among the designs in their pattern books are several that clearly had nothing to do with either clans or regiments. Titles such as Robin Hood, Caledonia and Wellington were chosen for their commercial appeal, and were changed or adapted as the situation demanded. Prior to 1820, for example, Wilson's marketed a tartan called Regent, which was obviously inspired by the Prince Regent (the future George IV). Once he had ascended the throne, this name no

▼ Caledonia was one of Wilson's evocatively named "fancy" tartans.

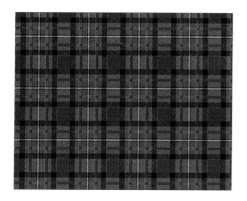

▲ *The Regent tartan was popular during the Regency period (1811–20).*

longer had a topical ring and was soon withdrawn. Despite this, the pattern itself remained in production and was eventually adopted as one of the MacLaren tartans.

Wilson's fancy tartans were often used to adorn such items as domestic furnishings or shawls. The latter were already becoming popular before the repeal of the ban on wearing tartan, largely because women were excluded from the ban. Wilson's made further attempts to capture the female market by producing tartan garments in a softer material made from the finest merino wool.

OTHER TARTAN MANUFACTURERS

Wilson's enjoyed a virtual monopoly in their field for many years. During the revival period, however, they faced competition from several other tartan manufacturers, perhaps the most notable being John Callander & Company of Stirling, who received commissions from no less a figure than George IV.

The city of Stirling itself gained a reputation as a weaving centre, and many workers joined the Incorporation of Weavers within the city, or the association of Country Weavers in the surrounding villages. For, as a commentator noted in the *Stirling Journal*: "Almost all the persons formerly engaged in the weaving of muslins…

have commenced the weaving of tartan, in consequence of its affording a better return for their labour."

ECONOMY TARTAN

Writing in the 1790s, John Lane Buchanan bemoaned the fact that, during the period of proscription, many Highlanders had lost the art of making their own tartan and had taken to buying cheap "Stirling plaids" instead. Sometimes, though, the weavers were not to blame for the quality of their goods. In army circles, it was not unusual for commanders to try to make a profit from the clothing they supplied to their regiment. For example, while the first colonel of the Black Watch, the Earl of Crawford, provided his men with two shirts and two pairs of hose each year, his successor, Lord Sempill, halved this allowance and made the plaids narrower to save on material. These penny-pinching ways may explain why English caricaturists of the period depicted Highlanders wearing ludicrously short kilts.

The most common form of economy when producing army uniforms was to use the cheapest and coarsest material available. This attitude was to

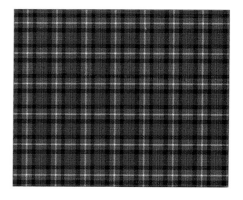

▲ *Wellington tartan honoured the achievements of the famous Duke.*

prove a long-running source of discontent that was only addressed in the 19th century through the intervention of Queen Victoria. In 1872, she noticed that the plaids of her Guard of Honour at Ballater were manufactured from a hard material and that "after a march in wind and rain the men's knees were much scratched and cut by the sharp edge of the tartan". Accordingly, she gave orders that "soft instead of hard tartan be in future supplied to Highland regiments".

▼ *A French print entitled Female Curiosity: the revealing nature of the kilt proved a popular comic theme.*

HIGHLAND UNIFORMS

The uniforms worn by Scottish soldiers made a significant contribution to the development of Highland dress. The standardization of setts was a new phenomenon, which exerted a great influence over clan tartans when they became fashionable during the revival period. Some elements of military attire also became popular in civilian circles, eventually becoming a routine feature of tartan outfits.

In spite of this, the English authorities made periodic attempts to change the Highland dress. From the outset, many pundits expressed doubts about its suitability for overseas campaigns. When Fraser's Highlanders embarked for North America in 1757, for example, it was suggested that the climate would prove too cold for the clansmen, and there were calls for the kilts to be replaced with something more practical. Colonel Fraser overruled these objections, much to the relief of his men. "Thanks to our generous chief," one veteran later recalled, "we were allowed to wear the garb of our fathers and, in the course of six winters, showed the doctors that they did not understand our constitutions; for in the coldest winters, our men were more healthy than those regiments who wore breeches and warm clothing."

THE KILT REPLACES THE PLAID

For civil servants in London, the kilt was certainly preferable to the belted plaid. This was largely a matter of cost, for once it became clear that the manufacture of a kilt required far less material than the older plaid, most regiments were obliged to accept it. Surprisingly perhaps, the garment did not prove a deterrent to recruits from other countries. When describing the Seaforth Highlanders in 1802, for instance, a commentator noted, "One-fourth of the men and officers were English and Irish, and three-fourths Scotch Highlanders and, singular as it may seem, the former were as fond of the kilt and the pipes as the latter, and many of them entered completely into the spirit of the national feeling."

It often seemed that the only exceptions to this rule were some of the

THE CHILDERS TARTAN
Pressure was put on the Highland regiments to accept a single, universal tartan. This reached a peak in the 1880s, when Hugh Childers, Secretary of State for War, commissioned a sett that he hoped would fulfil this function. Inevitably, this design (the Childers tartan) was strongly resisted, although it was eventually adopted by one of the Gurkha battalions. It was only in the 20th century that most elements of Highland dress were removed from the battlefield uniform and reserved for use on ceremonial occasions.

officers. Many of them preferred to wear trews, since they were more comfortable for riding, and used the kilt only on ceremonial occasions.

▼ *The 72nd Regiment was ordered to discard Highland dress in 1809, but was directed to resume it again in 1823.*

ACCESSORIES

The sporran evolved from a rather mundane civilian accessory. In essence, it was nothing more than a leather pouch, as can be seen in Waitt's portrait of Lord Duffus. In the hands of the military outfitters, however, this simple accessory was transformed into a flamboyant adornment that has since become an essential element of Highland dress. In some cases, sporrans were decorated with embroidered tassels or richly engraved clasps; at other times, they were decked out with tufts of badger fur. In certain parts of the world they were made of more exotic materials, locally sourced. In Canada, for example, the Frasers used raccoon skins to make their sporrans.

Headgear, too, changed dramatically. The old-fashioned flat bonnet was lined with a diced band of various colours. This design is thought to have been inspired by two coloured ribbons threaded in and out of slits in the cap, in order to make it fit more tightly on the head. In a very different vein, some Highland regiments began to wear much larger feather bonnets, similar to bearskins, and these were often adorned with a "heckle" (a plume) on the side. In most cases the heckle was white, but the Black Watch were entitled to wear a red heckle as one of their battle honours.

THE *CLOATHING BOOK*

Other details of military dress were set down in the *Cloathing Book*, which was first produced in 1742. This manual defined the minutiae of each uniform, right down to the spacing between the buttons, the style of the buttonholes, and the shape of pockets and cuffs.

The only omissions from the book were descriptions of the uniforms of officers. The main distinctions between their dress and that of the lower ranks were that their coats were scarlet, rather than red; they displayed decorative knots or aiguillettes on their shoulders; and they still wore a symbolic piece of armour in the form of a small, crescent-shaped gorget.

CEREMONIAL DRESS

As the threat of Highland rebellions receded, the bureaucrats in London lost interest in retaining the individualism of Highland dress. Instead, there were increasing attempts to bring the Scots into line with other regiments. Most criticism focused on the kilt, which was repeatedly described as too impractical a garment for use in some parts of the empire. In 1809, this resulted in seven regiments abandoning their kilts for trews or trousers, although the arguments still rumbled on.

▼ *The Kilmarnock bonnet was worn by soldiers serving with the Royal Scots between 1903 and 1939.*

▼ *This suit, in Ross tartan, is finished off by a sporran that was made from a complete animal pelt.*

▼ *Initially, sporrans were simple money-pouches, but military versions became increasingly large and ornate.*

▼ *The feather bonnet that was worn by the officers of 92nd Gordon Highlanders, around 1865.*

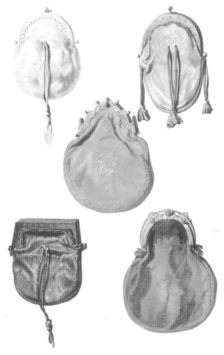

MILITARY PIPES

Nothing has been guaranteed to raise troops' spirits more effectively than the sound of bagpipes, and, in a way, this tradition can be traced back to the ancient Celts, whose warriors marched into battle accompanied by musicians carrying huge, animal-headed war horns. These would have emitted an ear-splitting noise when blown and the Celts probably hoped that the blaring din, which appeared to come from the mouths of monstrous creatures, would terrify their enemies.

THE FIRST BAGPIPES

Instruments similar to bagpipes were known in the ancient world, but it is unclear how they first developed in the Highlands. Some people believe that they evolved from the Roman *tibia* (mouth-blown double pipes), while others suggest that the Celts brought

▼ *The pipes were thought to date from Roman times, and are shown in this 15th-century miniature of Caesar crossing the Rubicon.*

them from their original homeland in the east. Either way, the pipes do not appear to have been combined with a bag until the Middle Ages, in an instrument known as a chorus.

There are early records of pipers at court, but the links with war do not seem to have occurred until the late medieval period. One of the earliest references relates to James IV's defeat at Flodden in 1513 where, according to tradition, the town piper of Jedburgh played his pipes on the battlefield. In spite of the carnage, he survived the conflict and handed the instrument down to his son; it was still in the family's possession in the late 18th century.

By the 17th century, references to bagpipes were more common. In 1645, for example, a piper tried to rally the Marquis of Montrose's royalist troops at the battle of Philiphaugh after they had been taken by surprise. Standing by the edge of a stream, the musician played until he was silenced by an enemy bullet. The spot has since become known as the Piper's Pool.

▲ *The Highland piper in this engraving by George Bickham plays an instrument with only two drones, while modern pipes have three.*

THE PIPER'S ROLE

The piper's role within the army was largely unofficial in the early days. The military authorities in the south regarded the drums, the fife (a high-pitched flute) and the bugle as instruments of war, but were slow to acknowledge the value of the bagpipes. The piper in one of the units of Mackay's Highlanders even had to hide his instrument on inspection days, while in many of the early regiments the piper was listed as a drummer on official records.

The first piper to gain proper recognition appears to have been Alexander Wallace, who became pipe-major of Dumbarton's Regiment in 1679. The standing of this rank has fluctuated over the years. Wallace himself was an officer, but in later years a pipe-major

was the equivalent of a sergeant (as indeed was a drum-major).

All regiments regarded their piper as an essential member of their team, building the morale of the troops on every occasion. The ruling Hanoverians came to realize this, so in the aftermath of Culloden they banned bagpipes, along with tartan. This was emphasized by the fate of James Reid, a piper in Ogilvie's Regiment, who was captured during the 1745 rebellion. At his trial, Reid pointed out that he had not wielded any arms during battle, but the judge dismissed his defence, pointing out that "a Highland regiment never marched without a piper...therefore his bagpipe, in the eye of the law, was an instrument of war". Reid was convicted and executed.

POPULAR TUNES

The music played by the regimental piper was very different from that of his civilian counterpart, who mostly played dance music. The army piper specialized in the *piobaireachd*, or pibroch, which assumed three main forms: these were stirring martial airs suitable for the

▲ *At the battle of Vimeiro in 1808, during the Peninsular War, George Clark continued to play his pipes, even though he was badly wounded.*

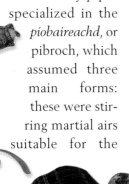

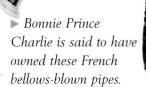

▶ *Bonnie Prince Charlie is said to have owned these French bellows-blown pipes.*

battlefield; marches to lift the spirits of soldiers on the move; and long, slow laments for funerals and other solemn occasions. For all of these, the piper frequently drew inspiration from historical events, so many pibrochs refer to battles. *The Desperate Battle* is thought to commemorate a clash at the North Inch of Perth in 1396, while *Black Donald's March to the Isles* relates to the battle of Inverlochy in 1431.

The greatest source of inspiration proved to be the Jacobite Rebellions, and a popular proverb of the time declared, "Twelve Highlanders and a bagpipe make a rebellion." The hopeful mood of the 1745 uprising was typified by *My King has Landed at Moidart*, a reference to Bonnie Prince Charlie's arrival in Scotland, while its sad aftermath was echoed in *Prince Charles' Lament*. Accounts of the uprising also make it clear that pipers accompanied the Young Pretender throughout much of the campaign. One source, for instance, described how "His Royal Highness made his entry into Carlisle seated on a

white charger and preceded by no less than a hundred pipers." This episode was later immortalized in the words of a popular song.

Over time, certain tunes became associated with individual clans and regiments. The Camerons, for example, liked to go into battle playing *Sons of Dogs, Come and I will give you Flesh*, while the Breadalbane Fencibles made use of *Lord Breadalbane's March*. Similarly, most units had their own tale of heroism, adding lustre to the honour of the regiment. At the siege of Badajos in 1812, for example, Piper MacLaughlan was in the forefront of an assault on the ramparts, playing a spirited rendition of *The Campbells are Coming*, when a shot tore through his bag and halted his playing. Undaunted, the piper calmly sat down on the nearest gun carriage and proceeded to repair his instrument, while the bullets fizzed around his head. Once this was done, he raised the pipes to his mouth and resumed playing.

MODERN TARTANS

WHILE RESEARCH INTO THE OLDER TARTANS CONTINUED IN THE 20TH CENTURY, THERE WAS ALSO AN UPSURGE OF INTEREST IN NEWER DESIGNS. EXPATRIATE SCOTS AND OFFICIAL BODIES RUSHED TO ADOPT THEIR OWN TARTANS, USING THEM TO STRENGTHEN TIES WITHIN THE GLOBAL SCOTTISH COMMUNITY.

THE KILT SOCIETY AND LORD LYON

By the start of the 20th century, the future of tartan was assured. Its history and traditions had been exhaustively researched and moves were afoot to formalize its role within society.

PRINCIPAL TARTANS

On the research side, the dubious impact of the *Vestiarium Scoticum* had been superseded by a swathe of less romantic, but ultimately more reliable

Previous pages: The Grampian mountain range.

▼ *Queen Victoria commissioned a series of portraits of her staff, dressed in Highland attire. Kenneth MacLeay's pictures, are perhaps the most lavish of all tartan illustrations. A surviving photograph of one of the models – Willie Duff – suggests that MacLeay romanticized his material considerably.*

publications on the subject of tartan. These included the *Authenticated Tartans of the Clans and Families of Scotland* by William and Andrew Smith, published in 1850, and the monumental, two-volume *Tartans of the Clans and Septs of Scotland* by W. and A.K. Johnston, first published in 1891. The latter featured more than 200 setts, many of which had never been illustrated before.

D.W. Stewart's *Old and Rare Scottish Tartans* appeared in 1893. It was far less comprehensive than the Johnston book, but has become a collector's item itself on account of its unique format. Instead of traditional illustrations it contained 45 miniature samples of actual woven-silk tartan. In complete contrast, Frank Adam's *Clans, Septs and Regiments of the Scottish Highlands*, first published in 1908, adopted a conventional format. It proved the

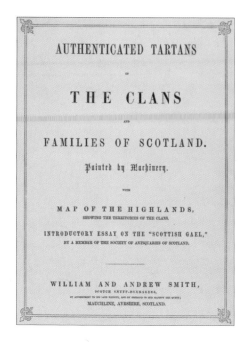

▲ *Each new publication added extra tartans. The snuffbox makers William and Andrew Smith used setts from the pattern books of Meyer and Mortimer, and Wilson's of Bannockburn.*

96

most comprehensive source book of the period, however, and was later updated by Sir Thomas Innes of Learney, the Lord Lyon King of Arms.

THE KILT SOCIETY

While various publications recorded the principal designs in use, other bodies sought to regulate the way the tartans were worn and who was entitled to wear each pattern. The Kilt Society (Comunn an Fheilidh) was founded in Inverness around 1902 to "encourage and perpetuate the wearing of Highland dress" and to this end members promoted their ideas during Wool Market Week – one of the busiest events in the city's calendar.

THE LORD LYON

Meanwhile, a system of registration was put in place under the auspices of the Court of the Lord Lyon King of Arms, the supreme authority on all matters relating to Scottish heraldry. The Lord Lyon is a minister of the Crown and a judge and, in many ways, his court operates like a normal court of law. He has considerable jurisdiction covering all aspects of ceremonial procedure

▼ *A badge with St Andrew, his cross, and the royal arms, which is associated with a Lord Lyon of the 1700s.*

during state occasions. His post dates back to the Middle Ages: the office of Lord Lyon was mentioned in records from 1318 and played a significant role in the coronation of Robert II in 1371.

The Lord Lyon holds his post directly from the Crown, although his precise powers were not set down until a statute of 1592 granted him full authority on the question of armorial bearings, enabling him to inspect and register the arms of the nobility. At the same time, he was also given the power "to put inhibition to all the common sort of people not worthy by the law of arms to bear any signs armorial".

The actual title of Lord Lyon King of Arms dates from 1662, and stems from the device of the lion that appears on the national coat of arms. Lord Lyon's post gained added powers in a statute of 1672, but these were short-lived, for in the wake of the Act of Union of 1707 the office went into a decline, becoming little more than a sinecure. The situation was eventually reversed following George IV's visit to Edinburgh in 1822, and the Lyon Court was reorganized by an Act of Parliament in 1867.

REGULATIONS FOR BADGES AND TARTANS

The Lord Lyon had close links with the Highland clans on account of the regulations governing crested badges, which were usually based on the arms of the chief. It was customary for the latter to give his followers a silver plate of the crest, which was traditionally worn as a bonnet badge. The badges took a number of different forms, in each case with the crest and motto displayed in a plain circlet. On the chief's badge, this would be surmounted by three tiny silver feathers. For a peer, a miniature coronet would be added. For untitled followers, the crest and motto would be depicted within a plain strap and buckle, showing that they were designated members of the clan.

▲ *The Lord Lyon precedes the Duke of Kent and Lord Provost in a procession in Edinburgh on Armistice Day 1934.*

The authority of the Lord Lyon over tartan developed as an offshoot of the regulations governing the style of badges. During the revival period, many clansmen had rushed to adopt their own tartan without establishing its pedigree. This resulted in considerable confusion and, in a few cases, different clans laid claim to the same tartan. By the time the tartans were recorded in print, it was often difficult to determine which clan had the best claim to a particular sett. Wherever possible, the Lord Lyon made a ruling on these cases and sought to avoid the problem occurring in the future by setting up a proper system of registration.

To enforce his authority, the Lord Lyon declared that only designs with the official approval of his court were in future to be known as tartans; the rest could be described only as "plaids". A list of all the registered tartans was included in Adam's *Clans, Septs and Regiments of the Scottish Highlands*.

Some of the registration duties were later passed to the Scottish Tartans Society, which was founded under the auspices of the Lord Lyon in 1963. This society also maintains its own cloth archive, which was based on the sizeable collection built up between 1930 and 1950 by two enthusiasts, James Cant and John MacGregor Hastie.

CLAN SOCIETIES

Just as tartans were being placed on a more formal footing with registration, the internal organization of the clans was being strengthened through the formation of clan associations and societies, which multiplied rapidly at the end of the 19th century. The idea was not new. The first clan societies dated back to the opening years of the 18th century, but their purpose and structure altered considerably over the years.

THE BUCHANAN SOCIETY

The first recorded club, the Buchanan Society, was founded in Glasgow in 1725. The initial stimulus appears to have been the publication of a book, *The History of the Ancient Surname Buchanan*, but, like a number of other early associations, the society became deeply involved in charitable works. A fund was set up to assist impoverished clansmen and to pay for the education or apprenticeship of their children. The members were also anxious to celebrate their most distinguished ancestors. In 1788 they raised funds to erect an obelisk to the memory of George Buchanan (1506–82), a former Keeper of the Privy Seal, who had been the tutor of the future James VI. The society was later granted its own coat of arms by the Lord Lyon in recognition of its achievements. It remains proud of its long tradition and still makes donations to worthy causes. Each new member is given a handbook, containing the names of every member since 1725 – some 2000 in all.

CLAN CHATTAN

The clan Chattan established its association in 1727. In this case, its primary concern was with the organization of the clan itself. Clan Chattan's unique structure – as a confederation of separate clans – led to ongoing fears about its dispersal. As a result, the leaders of the group engaged a number of lawyers "to watch and defend the interests of the clan against all who would seek the injury of any of the subscribers".

THE CLAN MACKAY SOCIETY

Following the foundation in 1759 of the Graham Charitable Society, which devoted most of its energies to the care of the needy, no further associations were formed until 1806, by which time the situation in Scotland had altered dramatically. The creation of McKay's Society (later renamed the Clan Mackay Society) was set against the looming shadow of the clearances. The first evictions had already taken place on Lord Reay's estates and there were fears about the clan's future. The aim of the Mackay Society was "to raise a fund for the mutual help of each of us in the time of afflictive dispensations".

One of the most significant aspects of the Mackay Society was the composition of its membership. In contrast with most Highland societies, which were often effectively clubs for the aristocracy or affluent professionals, the

◀ *The success of the 1888 Glasgow International Exhibition stimulated renewed interest in Highland tartans.*

▲ A military review during George IV's stay in Edinburgh, which prompted many clans to found their own societies.

Mackay association was dominated by tradesmen. The Preses, or chairman, was an undertaker, and his fellow directors included a grocer, a weaver, a vintner, a plasterer and a piper. In essence, they were ordinary clansmen struggling to provide the mutual protection that in former times they would have expected from their chief.

THE CLAN GREGOR SOCIETY

Formed under happier circumstances than the Mackay Society, the Clan Gregor Society was the next association to materialize, in 1822. The MacGregors had suffered greatly during the 18th century, when the whole clan was outlawed and their very name was proscribed. Once these measures had been repealed in 1775, the family were determined to recover their former prestige. Their good reputation

was largely restored at the time of George IV's visit to Edinburgh in 1822, when the MacGregors played a major role in the proceedings. Among other things, they provided the guard of honour when the Honours of Scotland, the royal regalia, were paraded from Edinburgh Castle to Holyrood Palace, and they formed part of the king's entourage during his subsequent processions through the city.

The Clan Gregor Society was founded in the euphoric aftermath of King George's visit. Ostensibly, the group's main aim was to generate and provide funds for the education of the children of needy clansmen. However, there was also a determination finally to lay to rest any vestiges of the stigma that had been associated with the MacGregor name for so long. Among the society's rules there was a significant passage stressing that "no person...who does not bear or will not resume the name of the clan...should be admissible as a candidate".

THE CLAN FRASER SOCIETY OF CANADA

A further innovation occurred in 1868, when the Clan Fraser Society of Canada was founded, long before its counterpart in Scotland. This was a reminder, if it were needed, that clanship matters were no longer exclusively a Scottish preserve. The Fraser association did not prosper at the time of its foundation, but was successfully relaunched in 1894. Invitations to its inaugural dinner were sent out as far afield as New York and Detroit and received around 300 replies.

The Clan Fraser Society of Canada was effectively the last of the early clan associations, which had developed sporadically over more than a century. The next phase was ushered in by the International Exhibition of 1888, staged in Glasgow. This influential show produced a surge of enthusiasm for Scottish traditions. As a result, almost 20 new clan societies were formed within the space of a decade.

HIGHLAND DRESS ACCESSORIES

As the identification and registration of tartans became more organized, so did other aspects of Highland dress. Members of the clan and Highland societies, who took such an interest in the minutest details of their traditional sett, found that there were a host of other items that required their attention. With the current growth in popularity of costume hire and specialist tartan shops, there is an ever-expanding list of accessories that may be worn.

CRESTS AND BADGES

The most traditional items of dress were, like tartan itself, concerned with the identification of the wearer. The clan crest, which is worn in the guise of a cap badge, enabled any observer to recognize not only the clan of the wearer but also his status within that body. In a similar vein, each clan was associated with a particular plant, a tiny sprig of which was attached to the cap behind the crest badge.

It is said that the sprig was intended to allow clansmen to identify their allies in battle, although in reality this theory hardly seems likely. Many of the plants chosen by the clans were very similar in appearance and were available for only a limited season each year, and in any event most clans used flags or banners as their rallying points in times of conflict. Nevertheless, the plant badge has given rise to an intriguing theory about one of the witches' prophecies in Shakespeare's *Macbeth* – when they assure him that he is safe until Birnam Wood comes to Dunsinane. In the play, the prophecy is fulfilled when Malcolm's troops cut down branches to use as camouflage. In fact, this could not have happened, since the battle took place in an open

▲ *The most elaborate sporrans were usually made of sealskin, with engraved decoration on the metal cantle.*

◄ *Military accessories adapted for civilian wear include the sporran, dirk, plaid brooch and belt plate.*

▼ *A silver shoulder-belt plate, worn by soldiers from the 1770s onwards. This one belonged to a Peterhead Volunteer.*

field, but it has been suggested that Malcolm's soldiers, as men of Atholl, might well have been wearing sprigs of rowan in their caps. In this sense, a "forest" of rowan could be said to have moved towards Dunsinane, giving rise to the legend.

THE SPORRAN

Among the accessories of Highland dress, the most celebrated item is the sporran. This started out as a simple leather pouch, and developed into the *sporan molach* ("hair sporran") in the 18th century. It was normally made out of goat, seal or badger skin (in Henry Raeburn's portrait of *The MacNab*, the gruesome sporran is formed out of the skin and fur of a badger's head). Fortunately, more environmentally friendly versions are now available. The metal mounting, or cantle, may be decorated with the clan crest.

In modern times the variety of sporrans has increased enormously, although they generally fall into three main categories – everyday wear (normally made out of leather and similar in many ways to the original sporran), semi-dress and dress.

▼ *The traditional black handle of this Highland* sgian dubh *includes the clan crest badge of the wearer.*

▲ *This 17th-century annular brooch from Tomintoul was used to fasten the plaid at the shoulder.*

DAGGERS AND DIRKS

The skean dhu, or *sgian dubh* ("black dagger"), is regarded as a traditional item, although it was not worn with any regularity before the 19th century. Its name probably stems from the fact that the handle was normally carved from black bog oak, although it may also refer to the implicit menace of the knife. In the past, it was usually carried as a concealed weapon and placed on show – frequently in the top of the stocking – only as a courtesy to a host. The original versions were often quite plain, but modern equivalents are frequently very showy. There may be a semi-precious stone set at the end of the hilt and the clan crest may be featured on a metal plaque.

Longer than the skean dhu, the dirk is and was always openly displayed. It became an accepted part of a military officer's uniform and can still be included in Highland wear today, but only on the most formal of occasions.

BROOCHES, KILT PINS AND OTHER FASTENINGS

If a plaid is worn, it can be attached at the shoulder with a brooch. The favourite format was the penannular brooch, which has a small gap in its hoop that is covered in interlacing and Celtic knotwork patterns. Brooches are

▲ *Queen Victoria gave this magnificent cairngorm brooch to John Brown, her controversial Highland manservant.*

now mostly worn by women, although they were originally used by men. Worn only by soldiers, shoulder-belt plates were first introduced into the British Army around 1770. They were metal badges displaying the regiment's name or number and were worn on the shoulder-belt, which was used to carry a sword, pouch or carbine.

According to tradition, the kilt pin which is fastened to the top apron of the kilt, was introduced by Queen Victoria, who ordered that her soldiers should be supplied with a fastening for their kilts after seeing a young recruit discomfited by a high wind. Kilt pins are worn decoratively, and can also be used for the display of a clan badge.

WAR SLOGANS

In addition to crests and plant badges, each clan had its own distinctive slogan or war-cry. The MacNeils, for example, adopted *Buaidh no Bas* ("Victory or death") as their battle-cry, while the MacDonells used *Dia's Naomh Aindrea* ("God and St Andrew"). Some of these slogans were registered with the Lord Lyon as part of a coat of arms.

THE DEVELOPMENT OF DISTRICT TARTANS

The decision to introduce a system of registration may have brought a sense of order to Highland dress, but it also left some people feeling excluded. Inevitably, many Scots no longer had a tartan that they could officially call their own. This was particularly true of those Lowlanders who had adopted a sett during the revival period and now regarded it as a symbol of their national identity. For Scots in this situation, district tartans offered a solution.

There is considerable evidence that the first district tartans developed at a very early stage and probably pre-dated clan tartans. It is unlikely, though, that there was any deliberate intention to create a sense of unity within a particular area. The patterns probably just reflected the personal preference of the weaver and his customers, and were to some extent governed by the locally available dyes and materials.

THE ARGYLL SETT

As clan tartans became more popular, the older district patterns fell out of use or were adapted into family setts. However, as Scottish surnames were frequently based on land, the two systems occasionally overlapped, as in the tortuous history of the Argyll tartan. This was included in Wilson's pattern book of 1819 and may be identical to

▲ *The rugged Grampian mountains cover much of the area of Argyll, in the western Highlands.*

the Argyll sett mentioned in their accounts in 1798. In later 19th-century sources, however, the pattern was identified as Campbell of Cawdor. This connection was logical, given that the Duke of Argyll was the Campbell chief. During the period between 1865 and 1881, the design was used as a regimental tartan, worn by the 91st Argyllshire Highlanders. Following their amalgamation with the 93rd Sutherland Highlanders, however, the tartan returned to its original function

as a district tartan. Once again, this was perfectly logical, since this was the area where the regiment had been raised.

IRISH DISTRICT PATTERNS

Prior to the modern period, a few district tartans had also been linked with places outside Scotland although, in each case, their precise origins are

▼ *The Argyll sett has served as both a district and a regimental tartan.*

▼ *Named after the seat of the Irish high kings, Tara dates to about 1880.*

▼ *The oldest Irish tartan, Ulster, was based on a historic garment.*

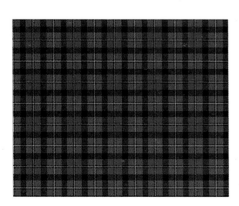

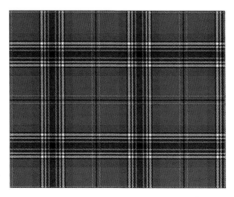

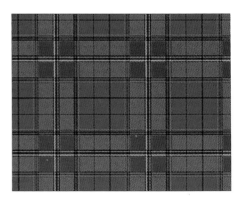

▲ *The Durham tartan was recorded in Wilson's pattern book of 1819.*

▲ *The Earl of St Andrews, initially a royal sett, is now a district tartan.*

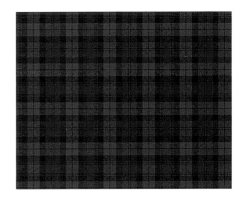

▲ *The Tyneside district tartan was originally meant for army use.*

unclear. There are, for example, three Irish district tartans that appear to be of some antiquity – Ulster, Tara and Clodagh. The Ulster pattern was based on fragments of clothing discovered in 1956 in a peaty ditch near Dungiven, in County Londonderry. Experts believe that the cloth scraps date back to the late 16th or early 17th century, and once formed part of a woollen cloak and a pair of trews. Their origins have remained a puzzle, however, since there is nothing to indicate how the clothing came to be there, or how it fits into the framework of Irish dress of the period. This has given rise to suggestions that the garments may have belonged to a Scotsman.

TRANSFERRED USAGE

The origins of the Durham tartan are equally mysterious. This design was recorded by Wilson's of Bannockburn in their pattern book of 1819. Wilson's were not averse to giving their patterns English names if they thought these might have a commercial or topical appeal, but there is no obvious reason why this should apply here. Instead, the general assumption is that the design was commissioned by a resident of the city or by someone bearing the surname. Either way, it has since been adopted as a district tartan.

This type of transferred usage was quite common. The St Andrews design, for example, was originally produced

for the Earl of St Andrews, but is now widely used by citizens of the Scottish town. Similarly, the Tyneside pattern was initially conceived as a regimental tartan, ordered by Lord Kitchener in 1914 for a new battalion, the Tyneside Scottish. The proximity of this English region to the Scottish border also made it suitable for use as a district tartan, however, and in recent years this has been its principal function.

MODERN CELTIC TARTANS

Within the British Isles, the number of new district tartans increased dramatically in the 20th century. One of the chief stimuli came from the growing ties between the various Celtic communities in western Europe. These have become increasingly determined to preserve the distinctive elements of their cultural heritage – in particular, their various tongues – while also

▼ *East Kilbride, a new town just south of Glasgow, uses this district tartan.*

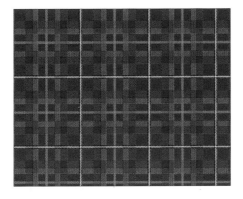

emphasizing their links with the broader Celtic community. As one of the most instantly recognizable symbols of Celtic culture, tartan was seen as the ideal means of cementing these bonds. Accordingly, setts have now been designed for Wales, Cornwall, the Isle of Man, Brittany and the Spanish region of Galicia.

The creation of the Welsh National tartan, using the colours from the Welsh flag, typified this trend. It was designed in 1967 by the Welsh Society in the hope that it would help the organization fulfil its stated aims – to be fully united with other Celtic countries, while retaining the individual character of Welsh culture, language and dress.

RECENTLY CREATED
SCOTTISH DISTRICTS

In complete contrast, some Scottish authorities have decided that tartan may be an effective way of promoting a sense of community spirit in areas that have no inherited traditions. It is notable, for example, that the development corporations of the new towns of Cumbernauld and East Kilbride wasted little time in commissioning tartans for their areas, hoping that these might produce a ready-made feeling of civic pride. Queen Elizabeth was presented with a rug bearing the East Kilbride tartan when she made an official visit to the town in 1990.

LINKS WITH THE NEW WORLD

Emigrant Scots played a significant role in the history of both Canada and the United States, and political and cultural ties with both countries remain very strong. In recent years, they have been reinforced by the creation of dozens of new tartans, re-emphasizing Scotland's ancestral links with the New World.

The waves of Scottish emigration were most evident in the 18th and 19th centuries and reached a peak in the middle years of Queen Victoria's reign. Upon their arrival in the Americas, most Scots tended to settle in communities alongside their fellow

▼ *Louis Dodd's painting shows the* Columbia *fur-trading in Nootka Sound, Vancouver, in 1787.*

countrymen. They also tried to join forces with their kinsmen and help each other wherever possible. The bonds of loyalty and clanship remained in force, even though the people in question were far away from their native land.

ST ANDREW'S SOCIETIES

Co-operation between emigrant Scots in America was channelled through a number of Scottish clubs that were generally known as St Andrew's Societies, although names such as Caledonian Society or Burns' Club can also be found. The organizations were similar in structure and function to the clan societies, although they were not restricted to a single clan.

Some of these bodies have a very long history. As early as 1657, a group of expatriates founded a Scots Charitable Society in Boston, modelled on a similar organization in London. This remained an isolated case until the 18th century, when such clubs began to proliferate. The first St Andrew's Society was formed in Charleston, South Carolina, in 1729, and a member of this group is said to have created the next, the St Andrew's Society of Philadelphia, in 1749. Similar bodies were founded in New York and Savannah, Georgia, in the 1750s.

With a few notable exceptions – an earlier Scotch Club in Savannah had been closely involved in politics – the groups were charitable organizations.

Most were restricted to Scots, though not all: the Charleston Society, for example, had some English members and pledged to "assist all People in Distress, of whatsoever Nation or Profession they may be."

As their membership became more prosperous, the societies functioned as dining clubs in addition to their fundraising activities. St Andrew's Day was a major event in the social calendar before it was superseded by Independence Day. Annual dinners were attended by many prominent citizens, including the governor, the chief justice and leading councillors.

AFTER INDEPENDENCE

The War of American Independence changed the fortunes of many Scottish emigrants. In spite of the difficulties they had experienced at home, many remained loyal to the British crown and, as a result, settled in Canada after the war – playing a major role in the fur trade, opening up new frontiers in the west, and assisting in the creation of the Canadian Pacific Railway.

The continuing strength of Scottish ties was echoed in regimental affairs. In the late 19th century, two new Highland units were raised in Nova Scotia – the Pictou Highlanders and the Cape Breton Highlanders – and both wore tartan uniforms. Even in the 1920s and 1930s, when several numbered regiments were reorganized, some were given very Scottish names

THE DEMAND FOR TARTAN

The maintenance of strong links across the Atlantic ensured a ready demand for tartan. In the 1820s a shipping firm offered to help Wilson's of Bannockburn export their goods, noting, "Tartans are much worn in America, and seen at all seasons, tho' best in the Fall; the patterns best adapted are large clan patterns…" The source of the pattern was less important. One New York retailer wrote to his supplier: "Never mind whether they are any known tartan exactly – that is not cared for here." This attitude would soon change. The International Exhibitions in Glasgow attracted over 5 million visitors in 1888 and more than 11 million in 1901, among them many Americans. The tartan warehouses' impressive exhibits prompted the creation of new clan associations and rekindled the enthusiasm of their counterparts in America.

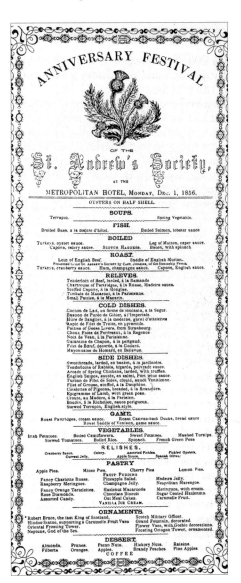

▲ *A lavish banquet was held in New York in 1856 to celebrate the centenary of the local St Andrew's Society.*

▲ *A print from* The Canadian Pacific *shows Scottish settlers heading west on the Canadian Pacific railway in 1915.*

– among them, the Canadian Scottish, the Cameron Highlanders of Canada, and the Lanark and Renfrew Scottish. All sported either kilts or trews.

A number of new initiatives have been taken to reinforce the ties. The Fraoch Eilean Canadian Foundation is a government-sponsored body that aims to promote "schemes and undertakings…for fostering and/or preserving Canadian and Scottish history and culture, in Canada and elsewhere", while Cassoc (Clans and Scottish Societies of Canada), set up in 1975, preserves clan traditions. Links have been forged through *The Clansman*, an Ontario-based magazine for all expatriate Scots, and the early inspiration for Tartan Day came from Canada. As a result, many Scots feel a closer kinship with Canada than with any other country.

AMERICAN AND CANADIAN TARTANS

Since 1831, when James Logan listed just 55 patterns in *The Scottish Gael*, the number of new tartans has steadily increased. Around 200 setts were identified by W. and A.K. Johnston in their *Tartans of the Clans and Septs of Scotland*, published in 1906, and close to 3000 tartans had been registered by the start of the new millennium.

A major reason for this increase has been the growing internationalism of tartan, as the diaspora of the Scottish clans has led to the creation of new

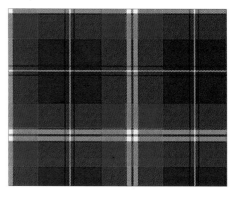

▲ *Many US tartans were created for public service departments, such as the New York Police Pipe Band.*

patterns around the globe. Inevitably, a high proportion of these have come from North America, where many Scots chose to settle.

DESIGNING MODERN TARTANS
The process began in earnest in Canada in the 1950s. Initially, most of the patterns were designed to commemorate

a landmark in the nation's history. The Prince Edward Island tartan, for example, marked the centenary of the Confederation Conference in 1964; the British Columbia celebrated the union with Vancouver Island in 1966; and the Canadian Centennial was one of several new tartans produced to coincide with the centenary of the Dominion of Canada in 1967. Several American tartans were introduced to mark the bicentenary of the USA in 1976.

The initial impetus behind the creation of many of these new tartans came from the scores of St Andrew's Societies that, over the years, had helped to bring together the descendants of expatriate Scots. The Illinois tartan, for instance, was commissioned by the local St Andrew's Society to mark the 150th anniversary of their foundation in 1840.

SYMBOLIC UNDERTONES
The creation of modern tartans offers considerable scope for innovation. During the revival period, clan chiefs had looked to the past for their setts, trying to restore a lost tradition. With a new tartan, however, designers can enjoy the freedom of working with a blank canvas. As a result, the patterns of many modern tartans have symbolic undertones, as weavers opt for colours

▼ *Prince Edward Island tartan was designed for an important anniversary.*

▼ *The British Columbia tartan was designed in 1966 by Eric Ward.*

▼ *The colours of Canadian Centennial symbolize Canada's natural resources.*

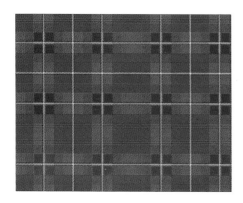

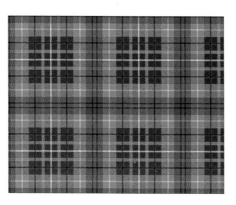

that have a particular relevance to their client. This symbolism takes many forms. Frequently, the heraldic aspect of tartan is maintained by merging the colours of flags and coats of arms. In American district tartans it is common to find the colours of the Stars and Stripes mingling with those of the St Andrew's Cross. At a local level, the US flag may be replaced by the state flag or the coat of arms of a city.

The topographical approach is almost as popular. Here, the colours represent local landmarks. Blue may stand for a river or a lake, green for a forest of pines, and yellow for a vast expanse of cornfields. In a few instances, the creators of the tartan have shown a great deal more imagination. When the District Fire Hall of the Caribou Islands in Canada was registering its design, for example, the inspiration for the colour scheme was outlined as follows: "Red for our sunsets, our lobsters and our fire trucks; white for our boats and our little white church; grey for the herring and the

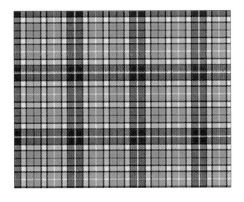

▲ *Caribou relates to an area strongly linked with Scottish emigration.*

▼ *This is one of five tartans that have been dedicated to Nova Scotia.*

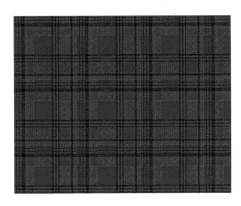

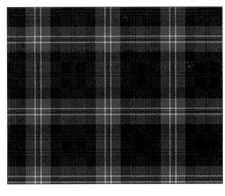

▲ *The Polaris tartan was designed for the US submarine base at Holy Loch.*

▼ *Designed for a naval base, the Edzell sett was later adopted by the US navy.*

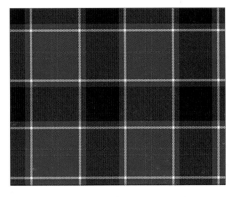

TARTANS FOR PIPE BANDS
In modern times, many public authorities, notably police and fire departments, have commissioned their own regimental tartans, with the aim of promoting a sense of brotherhood within the service. In most cases, the setts have been created for the use of the departmental pipe band. These groups often take part in public parades, such as those held on Tartan Day.

It is significant that many of the American pipe bands have Irish origins. The tartans of the New York Fireman's Pipe Band and the Metropolitan Atlanta Police were both commissioned by Emerald (Irish) Societies, rather than their Scottish equivalents.

seagulls." Similarly, the community of Sydney, Nova Scotia, chose to pay tribute to its leading industries. Thus the grey lines relate to the local steel plant; the orange refers to red-hot ingots; black stands for the coal in the furnaces; off-white for the limestone used in the production process.

OFFICIAL RECOGNITION
Whatever the size of the area linked with a tartan, American organizations are usually scrupulous about obtaining official recognition of their design. Perhaps conscious of the confusion that has sometimes arisen in Scotland, they take stringent measures to avoid any duplication. When a new state tartan is created, confirmation of its validity will often be sought through the state legislature. If more than one pattern is in circulation, the matter is occasionally resolved in the courts. A few tartan

designs have been copyrighted, though this can be counterproductive, since the retailers who have been excluded from using it will often seek an alternative tartan, which, through its greater availability, will eventually become the more popular design.

REGIMENTAL AND PUBLIC SERVICE TARTANS
Not all the new American tartans relate to states, provinces or cities. A high proportion have regimental overtones. Some were created for long-established services or military academies, which have a strong sense of tradition, while others are linked with newer forces that have a specific link with Scotland. The Polaris and Edzell tartans, for example, both relate to American naval bases. The Edzell base closed some time ago, but the tartan itself has now been adopted by the US navy.

A NEW APPROACH TO TARTAN

Traditionally, most tartans were associated with a clan, a district or a regiment. Beside these, "fancy" or trade tartans were used for decorative or commercial purposes. They gained very little coverage in the tartan surveys of the 1800s, but they had been in circulation since the previous century, when they were marketed by Wilson's of Bannockburn. In the 20th century the image and purpose of tartan were reinvented. Some of the older categories were expanded dramatically while, alongside them, entirely new concepts were introduced.

NEW THEMES

After World War II, when new patterns began to proliferate, other concepts appeared. The most common was the commemorative tartan, celebrating the anniversary of an event or body. Corporate tartans were used to promote firms or institutions, and charity tartans were used for fundraising. In addition, there was a veritable glut of other popular themes, among which were novelty tartans, sporting tartans, setts for non-military pipe bands and Highland games, and universal tartans.

There is a considerable degree of overlap between the various categories. Many trade tartans are named after places, so that they sound like district

TOURIST MERCHANDISE

Trade tartans fall into two camps: woven and non-woven. The latter are usually to be found on tourist merchandise, such as biscuit tins, trays and calendars. Even woven tartans are more likely to be found on rugs, shawls and blankets than on actual items of Highland dress. In many cases, the name of the tartan may not be made clear on the merchandise. Its only real purpose is to aid identification when the pattern is registered.

tartans, while some designs that carry the names of corporations or institutions are actually used only by their pipe bands. To complicate matters further, some tartans go through changes of name or function. Many commemorative tartans, for example, have a fairly limited shelf-life, so once the immediate anniversary for which they were created has passed they may be reassigned as district or universal tartans. This process is typified by a tartan that was produced for the Queen's Silver Jubilee in 1977. After the festivities were over, it lost its topical appeal and was renamed Holyrood.

FAMILY TARTANS

Some of the older categories of tartan have also been modified to reflect the changing times. For instance, some tartan enthusiasts who do not belong to any clan or sept have chosen to provide a sett for themselves and their family. Most of these relate to long-established Scottish names, but a few reflect more recent patterns of immigration. They include a number of Italian names, underlining the fact that many Italians – often former prisoners-of-war – settled in Scotland after 1945.

ASIAN TARTANS

A popular Sikh design was created in 1999, partly to mark the millennium and partly to celebrate the 300th anniversary of the Khalsa order. Its colours are drawn from the Scottish and Indian flags, while the structure of the design was inspired by one of the Campbell setts, which has been worn by several Sikh regiments. The pattern can be worn not only on kilts and trews, but also on turbans.

In the same year, the Singh tartan was commissioned by Sirdar Iqbal Singh, a retired businessman and the owner of a castle in Lesmahagow. He commissioned several portraits of himself proudly wearing his new tartan from his twin daughters, Amrit and

▼ *The Holyrood tartan was named after the royal palace in Edinburgh.*

▼ *The Italian tartan was designed for the use of Italians living in Scotland.*

▼ *The Singh tartan was commissioned in 1999 by Sirdar Iqbal Singh.*

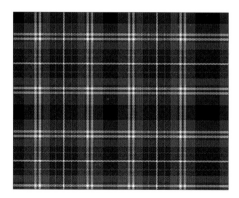

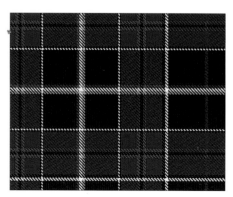

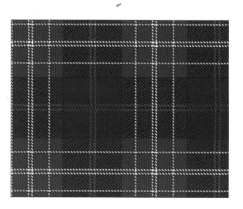

▲ *In this portrait of Sirdar Iqbal Singh by his daughters, Scottish-Asian links are wittily reinforced by the traditional weavers at the foot of the picture.*

Rabindra. Stylistically, these pictures resemble Indian miniatures, but as tartan portraits they belong to the same tradition as the canvases by Henry Raeburn and Richard Waitt.

The Singh tartan may be worn by anyone bearing the name, as well as any Asian with Scottish connections. As such, it has the same broad appeal as many of the older clan tartans. By con-trast, however, a growing number of modern family tartans are highly restricted in their use. These are private tartans, designed to celebrate a specific domestic occasion, such as a golden wedding anniversary or the union of two families through marriage.

TRADE TARTANS

The function of trade tartans has changed very little since Wilson's day, although the numbers involved have multiplied rapidly. The early examples often have a very romantic flavour, even if they do not always sound very Scottish. Robin Hood was designed to cash in on the vogue for outlaws, as was Gipsy, which was reputedly inspired by James Macpherson, a Scottish free booter who was the illegitimate son of a gipsy woman. Meg Merrilies was also named after a gipsy – a character in Sir Walter Scott's *Guy Mannering*. By the early 20th century, however, this reference had become so obscure that the pattern was listed as a conventional family sett.

In order to avoid this fate, most modern trade tartans are given much more general titles, such as Loch Ness, Niagara Falls, Harmony and Cavalier. Topical references are usually avoided, although there are some exceptions. The obvious example is the Stone of Destiny tartan, designed in 1996 after the Coronation Stone of Scone had been returned to Scotland having languished in England for 700 years.

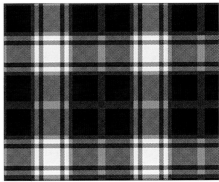

▲ *The fancy tartan Meg Merrilies was produced by Wilson's of Bannockburn.*

▼ *Despite its name, Niagara Falls is a trade rather than a district tartan.*

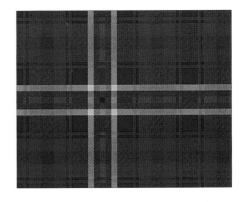

COMMEMORATIVE AND NOVELTY TARTANS

Among the newer categories of tartan, commemorative designs are probably the most common. The desire to celebrate an anniversary or an event has become one of the prime reasons for commissioning a new tartan.

ROYAL CELEBRATIONS
Some of the oldest commemorative designs are linked to royal events, such as coronations, jubilees and weddings. They were not always officially sanctioned; sometimes, private firms produced them to help sell merchandise relating to the event. One of the Coronation tartans, for example, was made at the time of George VI's coronation in 1936. It is known only from a sample in the MacGregor Hastie Collection, and there is no evidence to suggest that it ever gained royal approval. Technically, it is probably a trade tartan, although its origins remain a mystery.

SPECIAL OCCASIONS
Whether genuine or not, the existence of designs to mark royal events encouraged other institutions to follow suit. The celebrations for the Canadian centenary and the American bicentenary both spawned a number of commemorative tartan designs, which in turn paved the way for similar moves from individual American states and Canadian provinces.

Some tartans commemorate specific events such as the Olympics or the Commonwealth Games. For example, the Clanedin tartan was commissioned in 1970 to mark the fact that the Commonwealth Games were being held in Edinburgh. Tartans have also been produced for games staged outside the British Isles, although in such cases attempts are made to give the pattern a more lasting purpose. When the Olympic Games were staged in Barcelona, the authorities introduced a Catalan tartan. After the games, the sett became a straightforward district tartan – a practical response, although some might question whether there is any demand for such a tartan in Spain.

As commemorative tartans have proliferated, the links with Scotland are sometimes rather tenuous. There is, for example, a tartan commemorating the 400th anniversary of the sinking of the Armada in 1588. Here, the main

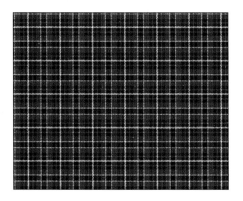

▲ *Coronation tartan appeared when George VI came to the throne in 1936.*

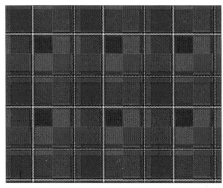

▲ *The Olympic tartan bears the games' emblem on each red block (not shown).*

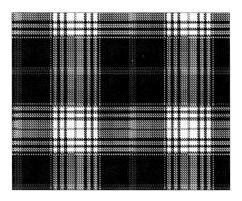

▲ *Hogmanay Plaid was designed to mark the millennial New Year.*

▼ *Clanedin commemorates the 1970 Commonwealth Games in Edinburgh.*

▼ *The red stripes of the Catalan tartan represent the blood of a local martyr.*

▼ *Scotland 2000 is one of a host of new designs for the millennium.*

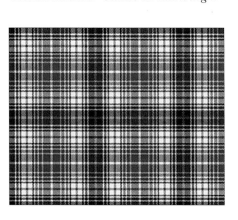

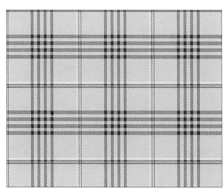

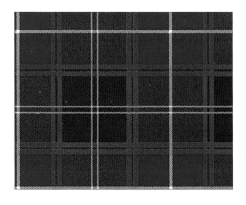

link is an old legend that some of the ships from the defeated Spanish fleet foundered in the Western Isles of Scotland, and that the shipwrecked sailors made a new home there.

On rare occasions, there is nothing more than a date to commemorate. A number of new tartans were introduced at the time of the millennium celebrations, among them the Hogmanay Plaid and Scotland 2000 setts. In cases such as these, where there is no obvious link with a district or a corporation, the design will probably either fall out of use or else become a universal tartan.

UNIVERSAL TARTANS

Tartans that can be used generally have grown in popularity largely because of their adaptability. Clothes-hire firms find them useful for customers who need to borrow Highland wear for a function, but have no particular links with Scotland. The same is true of film-makers, photographers and advertisers who want to convey a Scottish setting, while avoiding any specific clan associations. When the 1995 film *Braveheart* was being made, the producers took great pains to avoid using any recognizable clan tartans. Ironically, a Braveheart tartan already existed. It had been designed a few years earlier for a Japanese martial arts expert, who competed under this name.

The Scots have long had their own universal tartans: the Royal Stewart and Black Watch designs. However, these are appropriate only for people with UK connections and, even among Scots themselves, there are some who would prefer to avoid their royal or military overtones. A broader range of choice enables the wearer to find a design that has some relevance to their background. For example, when the boxer Mike Tyson was promoting a forthcoming bout in Scotland, he posed for the press wearing the American Bicentennial tartan.

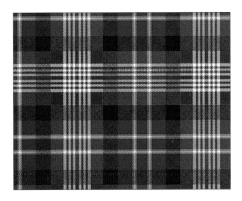

▲ *This US Bicentennial sett was renamed American (St Andrew's).*

▼ *A true novelty, the MacMedic sett was created for a first aid post.*

NOVELTY TARTANS

Many purists resent the use of tartan on occasions such as these, believing that it is undermining a key part of Scotland's heritage. Their real ire, however, is reserved for novelty tartans, which are currently on the increase. Some of these do, at least, display a laudable sense of humour. The MacMedic tartan, which is worn at the first aid post at the Stone Mountain Highland Games, adds a lighthearted touch that may well be appreciated by those who require medical help. At the games themselves, which are staged near Atlanta, the Georgia tartan is the favourite choice.

The sheer diversity of novelty tartans is extraordinary. The Balmaha tartan, for example, relates to a series of children's books about the Caledonian brown bear. It was produced for the clothing of the cuddly

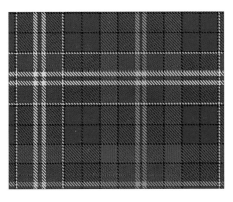

▲ *Produced for a range of teddy bears, Balmaha is based on the local scenery.*

▼ *Originally called Madonna, this sett is now known as Romantic Scotland.*

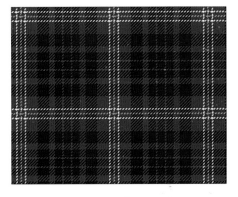

toys that accompany the books. The colours of the design represent the geography around Balmaha, which is a genuine place in the Loch Lomond region. In a very different vein, the Madonna tartan was commissioned as a tribute to the singer, who raised Scotland's tourist profile with her marriage to Guy Ritchie in Dornoch Cathedral in 2001. It has since been renamed Romantic Scotland.

Perhaps the least successful forms of innovation are those that attempt to team a tartan pattern with other motifs. The two most notable examples of this are the Olympic and the American with Eagle designs. The former has miniature versions of the Olympic emblem superimposed on each red block, while the latter features the United States heraldic emblem – a white-headed sea eagle – on every blue square of the design.

COMMERCIAL TARTANS

In recent years, the most significant development in the design and use of tartan has been the rapid growth of the corporate tartan. This is an enormously diverse field, which encompasses a wide variety of institutions, ranging from business concerns to government departments, from charitable organizations to pipe bands.

The motivation behind the development of the new corporate tartans is almost as varied as the bodies themselves, although it is fair to say that commercial instincts play a major role in their use. The new designs may be intended to promote a form of corporate branding, to create a clan-like cohesion between different departments of the same company, or to raise funds for a specific project.

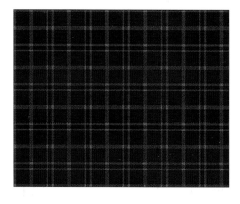

▲ *Highland Spring use two setts: one for still water, the other for sparkling.*

▼ *Irn Bru's tartan uses its packaging colours in a form of corporate branding.*

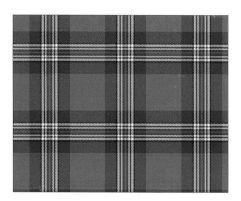

EARLY ADVERTISING

The rise of corporate tartans is a logical development from early forms of advertising. As long ago as the 18th century, images of Scotsmen in full Highland dress were already being used to market certain goods. Both in America and Britain, for example, the Scots were closely associated with tobacco and snuff. As a result, it was common to find wooden carvings of Highlanders serving as shop signs. These figures were invariably portrayed as soldiers, mainly because the kilt was chiefly a regimental garment during the proscription period, but also to avoid linking the product with any specific clan. The use of clan tartans remained a constant concern in later years, when Scots began to appear in illustrated advertisements, promoting a growing selection of goods.

BRANDING

It was always possible to keep the pattern vague, of course, but once the bandwagon of modern tartans gathered speed, it made more sense to jump on it. Accordingly, in the second half of the 20th century, many Scottish companies adopted their own tartans. For obvious reasons, the trend is most prevalent in industries that have a high Scottish profile. In international terms, the nation's most famous product is probably whisky. It comes as no surprise, therefore, to find that most, if not all, whisky manufacturers now have their own tartans. The makers of liqueurs and soft drinks have also followed suit.

As with other types of modern tartan, companies usually try to pick a design that has

▲ *Nairn's use of tartan underlines the firm's traditional values, century-long history and reputation for fine baking.*

◀ *In the 18th century, wooden images of Highland soldiers were often used to advertise snuff or tobacco.*

a special relevance to their product. Thus, in common with many district setts, the choice of colours in the design often has a symbolic association with the merchandise. In many cases, it is linked to the firm's packaging livery or its logo. For example, when the soft drinks company, Irn Bru, decided to launch their own tartan, they used the same shades of orange and blue that were already familiar to customers from the labels on their bottles.

MARKETING CAMPAIGNS

If a business does have a close connection with a particular clan, this will often be reflected in their choice of tartan. The history of Drambuie liqueur provides a case in point. According to the company literature, the recipe for this drink was handed down to the family who first produced it by Bonnie Prince Charlie. After his defeat at the battle of Culloden in 1746, the prince was sheltered on Skye by Captain John MacKinnon of Strathaird. When he escaped to France, Charles rewarded the captain for his protection by giving him the private recipe. As a result, the design of the Drambuie corporate tartan is closely modelled on the MacKinnon sett.

The pattern itself is mainly used for promotional purposes to emphasize the product's Scottish origins. This strategy is clearly aimed at overseas markets. Significantly, when Drambuie introduced its last series of "tartan" advertisements in 2001, the campaign was launched in Spain. The tartan was displayed in a humorous, modern context – the days of using images of Scotsmen in kilts have long gone. This emphasizes how, in global marketing terms, tartan is becoming increasingly detached from its links with Highland dress. The pattern alone, rather than its traditional applications, is now an instantly recognizable symbol of Scottishness worldwide.

NON-SCOTTISH COMPANIES

The use of tartan is not confined to UK companies. For, just as Scottish firms have employed their tartans when marketing their goods overseas, so foreign companies operating in Scotland have commissioned their own designs, to emphasize the strength of their commitment to the host nation and its workforce. Thus, the Swiss firm Forbo Nairn adopted a tartan when it opened up two factories in Scotland. Similarly, American Express produced a corporate tartan for use in its Scottish offices.

▲ *The American Express tartan is based on the MacWilliam sett.*

THE FASHION INDUSTRY

Corporate tartans are closely associated with clothing firms. Almost all the companies that make, sell or hire Highland dress have introduced their own designs. Familiar names such as Burberry, Aquascutum, Barbour and Pringle have all registered the checks and tartans that are uniquely associated with their products.

In some instances, clothiers have used their tartans to raise money for good causes. In January 2003, for example, Pringle joined forces with Amnesty International to raise money for the human rights organization. To mark Amnesty's 40th anniversary, Pringle launched a new range of fashion garments, designed by the couturier Russell Sage and featuring the Amnesty tartan. A percentage of the proceeds was donated to the charity.

Links between tartan and fashion have existed since the Romantic era, when French couturiers in particular used tartan in their designs, but they have increased dramatically since the boom in modern tartans took hold. The most celebrated examples are perhaps found in the work of Vivienne Westwood. Her 1993/4 Anglomania range included a tartan wedding gown, and her tartan bondage suits appear to have been inspired by the uniforms of Scottish regiments. With Jimmy Choo and Pringle, she took part in the "Tartan Fair" held at Isetan, a leading Tokyo department store, in 2003.

▼ *The three Drambuie designs are based on the MacKinnon tartan.*

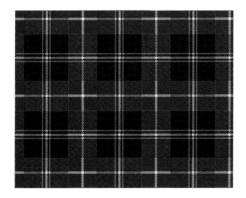

▼ *The distinctive Burberry check was introduced in 1924, as a coat lining.*

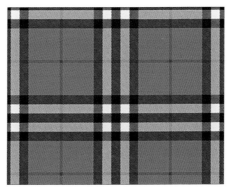

▼ *Aquascutum, founded in the 1850s, employs this familiar check.*

TARTANS OF CHARITIES AND INSTITUTIONS

The promotional value of tartan has become apparent to a broad spectrum of organizations, both in the public and the private sector, and they have helped to swell the ever-growing list of corporate tartans.

TOURISM AND HERITAGE

One of the most obvious applications for tartan is in the heritage-related industries. Several Scottish tourist boards have adopted their own designs, especially when they are launching joint projects. The United States tartan, for example, was produced by the tourist authorities in a bid to encourage more Americans to visit Scotland. The design features the colours from the flags of both nations. Similarly, the Chattahoochee tartan was commissioned by Scottish Border Enterprise in 1993 to mark the twinning of the Tweed and Chattahoochee rivers for tourism purposes. The Culture tartan was introduced in 1990, to coincide with Glasgow's status as the European City of Culture.

▼ *Gleneagles, opened in 1924, is one of Scotland's most famous hotels, renowned for its golfing facilities.*

▲ *A Highland parade launches the lively annual Scottish festival at the Queen Mary hotel in California.*

Corporate tartans have been linked with many popular tourist locations. The tartan of the National Galleries of Scotland underlines its official status by adapting the Black Watch or Government tartan, adding colours based on the architect William Playfair's original colour scheme for the gallery in Edinburgh. At the Gleneagles Hotel, the corporate tartan can be found on banners in the ballroom, as well as on a variety of merchandising. Its colours are even repeated on the hotel's distinctive fishing flies. But not

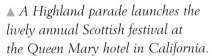

▲ *Queen Mary tartan was created for the old royal liner.*

▼ *Gleneagles tartan is one of two designs commissioned by the hotel.*

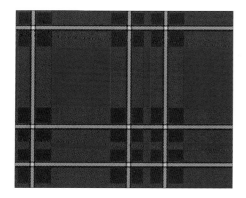

▲ *The Salvation Army tartan was commissioned by the Perth branch.*

▲ *The Diana Memorial tartan was launched in 1997 to aid her charities.*

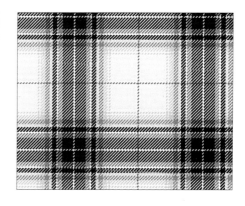

▲ *The Antarctica tartan raises funds for the British Antarctic Survey.*

all tourist attractions with tartans are in Scotland. In 1967, the liner *Queen Mary* was relocated permanently to Long Beach, California, and transformed into a tourist centre. It stages an annual Scottish festival to commemorate the land where it was built. The event is little short of a Highland games. There are sheep-herding demonstrations, whisky-tasting sessions, historical re-enactments and pipe-band competitions. The climax of the festivities is the Grand Tartan Ball, where the Queen Mary tartan may be worn.

TARTAN LIVERIES

The Historic Scotland tartan is used in a very different way. This is essentially a livery tartan, which can be worn by the custodians of various heritage properties, among them the guards in Edinburgh Castle. The notion of using tartan as a form of livery is very old, dating back to the days of the old Celtic courts, but it underwent a revival in the 19th century. When the great estates were rented out for hunting or shooting parties, staff were generally provided and some of these wore a set uniform. This could take the form of an estate check or tweed, or else the local tartan.

In the modern era, livery tartans are not confined to historical properties. They have also been used by airlines, such as Loganair and Business Air, and hotel chains such as Holiday Inn.

OFFICIAL BODIES

The popularity of corporate tartans has spread to official bodies such as local councils, churches and schools. Councils in Scottish have used new tartans as a way of forging links with councils in other countries through the twinning system. The Berwick Friendship and Elgin-Landshut tartans were both created for this purpose. Unlike most organizations, councils often choose the design of their tartans through an open competition, rather than by commissioning a professional designer.

Religious tartans are produced for a variety of bodies, ranging from specific churches, such as the Kirk in the Hills (a Michigan church modelled on Scotland's Melrose Abbey), to organizations such as the Salvation Army and the Baptist Union. The designs of these tartans often carry elaborate symbolic overtones. In the Salvation Army sett, for example, the red stripes symbolize the blood of Christ, blue represents the Heavenly Father, and yellow refers to the Holy Spirit at Pentecost.

Many universities and schools have acquired corporate tartans, although their reasons for doing so are very diverse. At Queens University in Ontario, the tartan represents the entire establishment, which was founded by Scottish Presbyterians, and its design has a precise, heraldic significance – it is based on the colours of the academic hoods of the six major disciplines. In contrast, the Oxford University tartan was produced specifically for the use of the students' Scottish Dance Society.

In many schools, the real impetus for adopting a new tartan comes from former pupils, who sometimes produce the design themselves. In one instance, however, Newton Primary, the tartan was actually created by the children as part of a project. At Hydesville Tower, an English school with Scottish owners, the tartan has been incorporated into part of the uniform.

MONEY-RAISING ACTIVITIES

In the modern era, the creation of new tartans has often been seen as a good way of raising money for worthy causes. Usually, this is achieved by selling a range of merchandise in the relevant pattern and then donating part of the proceeds to charity. Corporate, commemorative and district tartans have all been used for this purpose, and the range of charities is virtually endless. The most celebrated example, perhaps, is the memorial tartan created in memory of Princess Diana, which continues to raise funds for her favourite charities. In stark contrast, the Antarctic tartan was produced for the benefit of the British Antarctic Survey, which sponsors scientific studies in the region, and the UK Antarctic Heritage Trust, which aims to preserve the bases of early British explorers.

SPORTING TARTANS

One of the most remarkable modern developments of tartan has been its expansion into areas that are far removed from the traditional themes of clanship or the land. Sports-related tartans have proved particularly successful, perhaps because, in some eyes, the bonding between fans is as close and passionate as any family ties.

FOOTBALL

In the UK, anyone who starts a search for "tartan" on the internet will find that more than half the sites are devoted to the Tartan Army. This term dates from the 1970s and describes the supporters of Scotland's sporting activities, although it is most associated with the national football team.

The Tartan Army sett was an immediate success in 1997, and has been in evidence at World Cup events ever since. It features on traditional items, such as scarves, but has also been used to good effect on some outlandish

▼ *A happy football fan wears a "See you Jimmy" hat and wig, with the Scottish flag painted on his face.*

▲ *Part of the course at St Andrews, the home of golf, with the Royal and Ancient clubhouse in the background.*

accessories, which were playful parodies of Highland dress. These include the "See you Jimmy" hat (a type of cap attached to a bright orange wig) and giant "bunnets" (huge bonnets or "tammies", adorned with pheasant feathers).

Predictably, many individual football teams have acquired their own tartans. The two biggest Scottish clubs – Rangers and Celtic – took this step in the late 1980s, and most of their rivals followed suit. In most cases, the design is loosely based on the team's playing colours. In keeping with the growing internationalism of tartan, there is even an overseas team with its own sett – Hammarby IF, which won the Swedish Championship in 2001.

GOLF

While football is Scotland's national game, the country is probably better known in many quarters for its association with golf. The Scots are said to have invented the game in the 14th or 15th century. It soon became immensely popular. Indeed, in 1457 James II of Scotland banned the game, because he felt it was distracting too many of his subjects from their archery practice. The first organization, founded

▲ *The tartan of The St Andrews Old Golf Course Hotel and golf resort.*

▼ *The similar Royal and Ancient sett is restricted to members of the golf club.*

in 1735, was the Edinburgh Golfing Society (now the Royal Burgess Golfing Society of Edinburgh), but its fame was eventually eclipsed by the Society of St Andrews. Formed in 1754, this body encountered some early problems, notably when the links were sold off to a rabbit farmer in 1799. It was responsible for reducing the standard golf course from 22 to 18 holes and went on to become world famous after gaining the king's permission to change its name to the Royal and Ancient Golf Club of St Andrews in 1834. Its reputation was further enhanced in 1897, when it was recognized as the principal authority on the rules of the game.

Given Scotland's prominent role in the sport, it is hardly surprising that

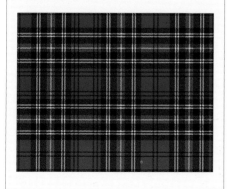

THE TARTAN ARMY
Keith Lumsden, of the Scottish Tartans Society, designed the Tartan Army sett in 1997 by incorporating elements from the Royal Stewart and Black Watch designs. These were chosen because both are universal tartans, that is, tartans that can be worn by any Scot. As the sovereign's tartan, Royal Stewart can be worn by any of the Queen's subjects, while the Black Watch design was early on classified as the Government sett.

▼ *Although mainly associated with football, Tartan Army can be worn by supporters of any Scottish team.*

▲ *The Callaway tartan is a modern design for a golf course in California.*

there are many golf-related tartans. The emphasis is very different to football, however, since most golfing tournaments revolve around individual competitors, so the wearing of team colours is not appropriate. The commercial purpose, too, is often quite dissimilar. The Royal and Ancient tartan, for example, was introduced in 1993 as part of a fundraising project to help restore some of the club's historic buildings. The design proved such a success that it is now used on a bewildering range of accessories, from jackets and baseball caps to tee bags and visors.

Often, the tartan is linked to a specific tournament, rather than a club or a course. The Hilton Champion design, for example, was commissioned specifically for the MCI Classic – the Heritage of Golf tournament (recently renamed the WorldCom Classic – the Heritage of Golf), which has been running for more than 30 years at Hilton Head Island in South Carolina. The tournament organizers have always been keen to stress their affinity with the old country: the competition is played on a Scottish-style links, and it raises money for charitable causes through membership of the prestigious Tartan Club. The most visible connection with Scotland, however, is the prize awarded to the winner of the tournament – a tartan jacket.

Among other golfing designs, there are tartans for the Kingsbarns golf club,

which is connected to St Andrews, and the Callaway sett, which was produced for a course in Carlsbad, California. One of the most widely used patterns is the Golfers tartan, for anyone with an interest in the game.

OTHER SPORTS
There is a scattering of tartans relating to sports other than football and golf. The London Scottish Rugby Club design is self-explanatory. Bowlers is both a sporting and a commemorative tartan: it can be used by anyone involved in the sport of bowls, although it was specifically designed to celebrate the 700th anniversary of the game, which coincided with the 2004 World Bowls Championships.

Most tartans relating to athletics fall into a similar category, since they can usually be linked with a particular Olympics or Commonwealth Games.

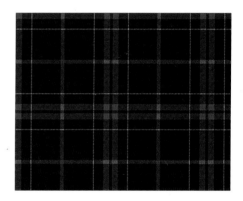

▲ *London Scottish Rugby Club tartan is for club members and employees.*

▼ *The Bowlers tartan commemorates the 700th anniversary of the sport.*

HIGHLAND GAMES

Once to be found only in Scotland, Highland games are now enjoyed in many parts of the world, and these colourful competitions have contributed to the growth of the international interest in tartan.

Numerous attempts have been made to find historical precedents for these contests. In ancient times, the Celts staged funeral games in honour of their gods. The most famous of these were held at Tailtiu (Teltown) in Ireland, where the main events appear to have been horse-racing and martial arts, although the festival also had religious overtones. In Scotland itself, Malcolm Canmore (who took the throne as Malcolm III, r.1058–93) used to summon clansmen to the Braes of Mar, where "by keen and fair" contest they could demonstrate who would make the best soldiers in his army.

The modern Highland games can be traced back to the 18th century. In 1781, the Falkland Tryst held the first Highland Society Gathering, although the main focus of the event was a piping competition rather than athletics. A more conventional programme was introduced at St Fillans in Perthshire in 1819. The idea of the Highland games really took off in the 1820s, however, following the success of George IV's state visit to Scotland.

THE BRAEMAR GATHERING

The most famous of the early games, the Braemar Gathering has its roots in the Braemar Wright's Friendly Society, formed in 1816. A decade later, this was reorganized as the Braemar Highland Society, which staged the first competitive events in 1832. They came to real prominence through the patronage of Queen Victoria. At Laggan in 1847, she had enjoyed watching the games that were arranged in honour of Prince Albert's birthday, and she paid her first visit to

◀ *Tossing the caber is always the most popular of the "heavy" events at Highland games.*

Braemar the following year. Before long, she was a regular visitor and became the games' chief patron, donating money for prizes and occasionally hosting the event at Balmoral Castle.

By the end of Victoria's reign, similar events were being staged in other parts of the country, and their popularity grew during the 20th century. In 2003, there were no fewer than 92 gatherings held in Scotland.

TOSSING THE CABER

The programme of activities at individual gatherings varies, although the main focus of attention is usually on the so-called "heavy" events. The most famous of these is tossing the caber. The origins of this contest are not

▼ The Illustrated London News *showed Victoria and Albert enjoying the Laggan Games in 1847.*

▶ *Initially, a sledgehammer or smith's hammer was probably used for throwing the hammer.*

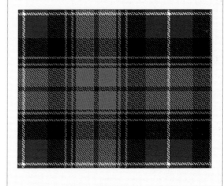

entirely clear, although most authorities believe that it was invented by foresters, who sometimes had to throw felled pieces of timber across small streams. The caber itself is a natural tree trunk and, as such, its dimensions vary. In *The Guinness Book of Records*, a maximum length of 7.6m/25ft and a weight of 127kg/280lb have been cited, but more realistic average dimensions would be 5.1–6.1m/17–20ft, at a weight of 59–68kg/130–150lb. In some places, the caber is left to soak in a loch or has molten lead poured into tiny boreholes prior to the contest, in order to keep the weight at a suitable level,

▼ *A shot putter hurls his shot at the Orange County Fair in California, one of America's many highland gatherings.*

since timber becomes lighter as it dries out. Contrary to popular belief, the contest is not decided on the length of the throw. Rather, the feat is meant to test the control of the competitor, and the winner is the man who manages to hurl the caber in the straightest line.

POPULAR EVENTS

Among the other trials of strength, the tug-of-war and the hammer-throwing competition are generally major attractions. Originally, the shot was a large stone and varied in size at different venues: at Tomintoul, for example, it weighed 5.9kg/13lb, while that used at Braemar was a massive 12.7kg/28lb. These power contests became popular because they often pitted local blacksmiths and farriers against trained soldiers. Alongside the athletic events, most gatherings also feature competitions and displays of pipe bands and Highland dancing.

WORLDWIDE GAMES

In recent years, Highland games have been staged in other parts of the world, most notably in North America and the Far East. In the USA, the trend was pioneered by North Carolina's Grandfather Mountain Games, which were founded in 1956. The initial impetus came from Donald MacDonald, who had attended the 1954 Braemar Gathering and determined to recreate its spirit in his homeland. "Armed with my Braemar souvenir programme and set of rules," he wrote, "we set about designing and staging 'an American Braemar'. I selected 19 August as the date, because it commemorated Glenfinnan and the raising of the Prince's standard, which was primarily the start of the downfall of the Highlands, and caused our people to go to North Carolina in the first place." To emphasize this connection

THE COWAL GATHERING TARTAN

Most Highland games do not have their own tartan, but in 1994 the Cowal Gathering commissioned a new tartan to mark its centenary. The gathering takes place at the end of August, and is held at Dunoon. The colour scheme of the design is dominated by blues, representing the neighbouring lochs, and greens symbolizing the mountains of Argyll.

▼ *The Cowal tartan features on merchandise ranging from kilts and scarves to ties, shawls and rugs.*

with the Jacobite rebellion even further, the prizes at the inaugural games were presented by the guest of honour, the great-great-grandson of the Scottish heroine Flora MacDonald.

In the overseas games the programme of events is often slightly different from those in Scotland. At many gatherings there is an "avenue of the clans", where visitors can learn more about their Scottish ancestors. In addition, there may be cattle shows, storytelling areas, parades of vintage cars, sheep-dog demonstrations and historical re-enactments. The most spectacular innovation of all, perhaps, is the finale at the Highlands of Durham Games in Canada, where – inspired by the traditional festivities of Up-Helly-Aa in Shetland – they burn a replica Viking longship.

SCOTTISH DANCING

In recent years dancing has provided one of the most obvious reasons for donning kilts and tartans. In competitions, demonstrations or at social events, the wearing of Highland costume has become an essential element of traditional Scottish dancing, whether it is Highland dancing or Scottish country dancing.

HIGHLAND DANCING

According to some authorities, Highland dances are ultimately derived from the ritual mime dances of the Picts. Today, these traditional dances are mainly seen only in the competitions or demonstrations at gatherings for Highland games.

There are four principal dances, each with its own colourful set of associations. The *Sean Triubhas* (Old Trews) is meant to portray a Highlander shaking off his English trousers in disgust during the period when the wearing of the kilt was outlawed. The Reel of Tulloch is said to have been created by accident

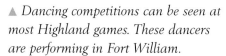

▲ *Dancing competitions can be seen at most Highland games. These dancers are performing in Fort William.*

▼ *In this photograph of around 1900, dancers stage a Reel of Tulloch for the benefit of the cameraman.*

by the villagers of Tulloch in Inverness-shire. One Sunday morning, when the weather was particularly cold, they were waiting outside the church for their minister to arrive from the next parish. He was delayed, however, and so, in order to keep warm, the congregation started to clap their hands and stamp their feet on the ground. This eventually developed into the frantic dance that is performed today.

THE HIGHLAND FLING

Probably the most famous of the Highland dances is the Highland Fling. According to one story, it was created in 1792 in honour of Jean, Duchess of Gordon, for the part she played in raising the Gordon Highlanders. More prosaically, it has also been said that the dance originated when a shepherd boy tried to mimic the graceful movements of a stag's antlers with his arms. Unusually, the Highland Fling is performed on a single spot. This is said to have occurred because Highlanders liked to show off their skill by performing the entire dance on the surface of their targe, or shield, without allowing their feet to touch the ground.

THE SWORD DANCE

Performers require equally nimble feet when attempting the Sword Dance, or *Gille Calum*. According to legend, the dance was invented by Malcolm Canmore (eventually Malcolm III),

after his victory over Macbeth at either the battle of Dunsinane in 1054 or at Lumphanan in 1057. After the conflict, Malcolm is said to have placed two swords on the ground, to form the sign of the cross, and then danced for joy in between the blades. As an extension of this apocryphal tale, clansmen were said to have repeated his feat prior to other encounters, as a form of war-dance. If they managed to complete the dance without touching the blades, this was seen as a good omen for the coming battle.

SCOTTISH COUNTRY DANCING

Also to be seen at Highland games, Scottish country dancing has developed into an independent pastime that can be enjoyed all the year round. It has strong links with folk dancing, even if the "country" tag should be used with caution. In some ways, it might be more accurately described as "contra-dancing", from the formation that is adopted in many of the numbers, where the dancers line up facing each

▲ *A vignette on the sheet music for* Danses Calédoniennes *shows children performing for Queen Victoria.*

other. It would also be wrong to assume that the current repertoire stems purely from the kind of dances that were once enjoyed by peasants. On the contrary, many elements appear to have come from courtly dances, and in the past, Scottish country dancing was enjoyed by all levels of society.

The dances themselves have an international flavour. When they were employed as mercenaries, Scottish soldiers took them to many parts of Europe, where they were modified by local influences. Indeed, one of the basic steps in many Scottish dances is the *pas de Basque*, which originated in the Pyrenees region.

TELEVISION PHENOMENON

In the UK, Scottish country dancing was popularized by a television show, *The White Heather Club*, produced by the BBC for over a decade at its Glasgow studio. The winning combination of song and dance in full tartan attire lasted for over 285 editions between 1958 and 1968, gaining impressive audience ratings and undoubtedly introducing many people to the activity. Eventually, the show's

unvarying format staled, however, and may have helped to give tartan an old-fashioned image in Britain.

A WORLDWIDE FOLLOWING

The most important contribution to Scottish dance has come from its governing body, the Royal Scottish Country Dance Society, which was founded in 1923 and has spread the gospel about Scotland's traditional dances to an international audience. Above all, this has been done through the medium of the society's summer schools, which are held at St Andrews and attract students from all over the world. The schools were organized for many years by a co-founder of the society, Jean Milligan, who was nicknamed "the First Lady of the Dance". After her death, a Strathspey (a dance with gliding steps, slower than a reel) was named after her, in honour of her inspirational achievements. The society has encouraged the foundation of many overseas branches and centres now flourish as far afield as Toronto, San Francisco, Tokyo, Sydney, Nairobi and the Hague.

▼ *With their competition numbers on their kilts, these women are performing a nimble version of the sword dance.*

DANCE SETTS

If dancers belong to a recognized clan, they will normally wear their traditional dress tartan. Many dance enthusiasts fall outside this category, however, and a number of modern tartans have been created for their benefit. For example, the Katsushika Scottish Country Dancers of Japan have registered their own tartan, as have the Scottish Dance Club at Leeds University and the dancers at the Aboyne Highland Games. In some places, new tartans have been shared by dancing and piping associations, as is the case with both the New Zealand and the South Canterbury Centre setts.

FAR EAST ENTHUSIASM

The use of tartan and the creation of new designs have increased dramatically in areas affected by past waves of Scottish emigration – notably North America and the Commonwealth countries. A more surprising development, though, has been the surging popularity of tartan and Scottish dance in the Far East, where the influence of the Highland clans was very limited.

TAIWAN AND SOUTH KOREA

This popularity can be discerned from the number of retail outlets and franchises that tartan suppliers have opened up in places such as Taiwan, Japan and South Korea. The trend began in Japan in the 1990s and has mushroomed. Previously, Scottish firms tended to market their goods in Asia under a "Best of British" umbrella, but the marketing now has a distinctly Scottish flavour, with the emphasis on Highland culture. A spokesman for Kinloch Anderson, a leading Scottish company in this field, recently commented on their expansion into Korea: "Of course, we are majoring on the heritage behind Scottish dress, but it is not a clan-affiliated push, such as you might employ in the US or the Commonwealth."

▲ *A piper at the Jakarta Highland Gathering, where there are solo competitions for pipers and drummers.*

SCOTTISH DANCE IN JAPAN

The profile of Scotland's heritage has been raised by the spread of such activities as Highland

▶ *The Java St Andrews Society holds a ceilidh in the run-up to the Jakarta Highland Gathering.*

games and Scottish country dancing. The latter, in particular, has become extremely popular, leading to the creation of several overseas branches of the Royal Scottish Country Dance Society (RSCDS).

In the 1950s, two members of Japan's Folk Dance Federation – Mr Shimada and Mr Nakayama – became the first Japanese visitors to attend the summer school in St Andrews. Their lead was followed by Mr Hiroyuki Ikema, who has played a major role in popularizing Scottish country

dancing in Japan. Educated in Tokyo and New York, Mr Ikema is a gymnast, teacher and the author of *Folk Dance in Japan*. During a visit to the USA in the late 1960s, he met Jean Milligan, a co-founder of the RSCDS, and rapidly developed a fascination for Scottish dance. After returning home to Japan he became the driving force within the Tokyo Metropolitan SCDS and ran a highly successful series of classes. The

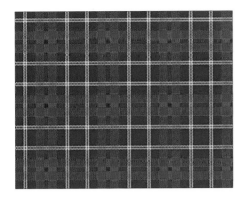

▲ *This sett was designed for a Tokyo-based country dancing team, the Katsushika Club, in 1995.*

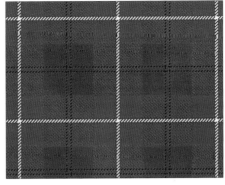

▲ *The Kansai Highland Games tartan was registered by the games' organization in 1999.*

ers also try to bring over performers from Scotland. At the 2003 games, for example, the Kirkwall City Pipe Band was invited to make the 27-hour journey from the Orkneys to take part in the festivities.

group met several times a month and hosted an end-of-year party, which attracted over a hundred performers, with all the male dancers attired in traditional kilts.

Mr Ikema founded the official Tokyo Branch of the RSCDS in 1984, and his local group, the Katsushika Scottish Country Dance Club, was established two years later. The club's members take their dancing seriously and many attend RSCDS summer schools at St Andrews or in Canada. With so much enthusiasm, it is hardly surprising that the Katsushika Club has performed well in competition. In 1993, it won 3rd prize in the Scottish Country Dance section of the Mikasa-no-miya (Royal Family) Competition and, four years later, it gained 1st prize in the contest at the Tokyo Highland Games.

HIGHLAND GAMES

Many Far East Scottish country dancing clubs enjoy competing in locally held Highland games. At present, only two of these events have secured their own tartan – the Kansai Games in Japan and the Jakarta Highland Gathering in Indonesia – but the taste for these contests is spreading fast and there is little doubt that others will follow in the future.

Jakarta has two tartans, both of which come under the aegis of the Java St Andrews Society. The hunting sett

is used by the society itself, while the dress tartan is reserved for the dancers performing at the local Highland gathering held in September. Scottish country dancing forms a major part of the group's social activities.

THE KANSAI GAMES

As in Jakarta, the Kansai Games, which were founded in 1989 by Maud Robertson Ramsay, have separate tartans for the games and the local St Andrews Society. The games themselves feature most of the standard contests, along with homelier items such as beetle drives, egg-and-spoon races and a "wellie" toss. The organiz-

KIRKIN O' THE TARTAN

An unusual aspect of some of the highland games around the world, including the Kansai Games, is the continuation of the old custom of a Kirkin o' the Tartan church service. This was a tradition originally established for the families of Scottish soldiers serving overseas, and perhaps dates as far back as the 1500s. While he was away fighting, a soldier's wife would take a sample of the family tartan to the kirk, or church, to have it blessed by the minister, and would pray for his safe return. The custom of kirking the tartan is still maintained by certain Scottish communities around the world, in particular North America, where it is seen as a way of blessing the clan or family. Ironically, it is no longer practised in Scotland itself.

▼ *The annual Jakarta Highland Gathering includes a display of massed pipes and drums.*

TARTAN'S FUTURE

If there were ever any doubts that tartan could maintain the same high levels of interest that it inspired in the past, these were dispelled during the resurgent period after the Second World War. At the Festival of Britain, which was staged in 1951, the nation shook off the despondency of the war years and celebrated in style. Tartan played a major part in these festivities.

In Scotland, the main focus of the 1951 festival was a huge Gathering of the Clans, which took place in Edinburgh over a period of four days. The events included grand balls, Highland games and pipe-band competitions but, for many people, the highlight was a spectacular parade down Princes Street, in which 1000 pipers took part.

THE EDINBURGH FESTIVAL
The taste for this kind of display had already been created by the recently established Edinburgh Festival. Its earliest events date back to 1947, but the Edinburgh Tattoo was introduced in 1950, under the auspices of Brigadier Alasdair MacLean of the Queen's Own Cameron Highlanders. The Tattoo forms the climax to the festival. It features some dramatic elements

▲ *The grand finale of the military tattoo in Edinburgh in 1952 took place on the floodlit Castle Esplanade.*

interspersed with folk dancing, gymnastic displays and musical interludes by military bands from around the world. The most impressive sight of all, however, is presented by the massed pipes and drums, in full Highland regalia, parading under the ramparts of the castle.

TARTAN DAY CELEBRATIONS
Spectacles similar to the Edinburgh tattoo have been seen at various Highland games, where there is usually a pipe-band competition. In recent years, however, these have been upstaged by the growing popularity of the Tartan Day celebrations. In just a few years, this event has grown into a genuine phenomenon that threatens to become the most significant date in the Scottish calendar. Like "kirking the tartan", it is a tradition that has developed outside Scotland rather than within it.

The initial impetus came from Canada. In 1987, Nova Scotia held its first Tartan Day as a tribute to the achievements of those of its citizens who had Scottish roots. The event proved a success and there were moves to extend it to other parts of the country. Then in December 1991, at the instigation of the Clans and Scottish Societies of Canada, Ontario followed

▼ *With the castle as a magnificent backdrop, the tattoo is a spectacular climax to the Edinburgh Festival.*

suit. Soon all the provinces had become involved, with the exception of Quebec and Newfoundland.

It did not take long for a similar momentum to build up south of the border. In March 1998, the US Senate passed a resolution confirming 6 April as National Tartan Day. The date was

NEW YORK'S TARTAN DAY PARADE

In 2002 around 7800 pipers and drummers took part in the Tunes of Glory procession down Manhattan's 6th Avenue – not far short of a world record. The chief guests of honour were Sean Connery and Scotland's First Minister, Jack McConnell. A new tartan – New York City – was specially produced for the occasion. Its colour scheme included a pale blue for the Hudson River; a deeper blue for Scotland's flag; green for the Scottish countryside; red for a local charity (Gilda's Club Worldwide); and black for the victims who lost their lives on September 11.

▲ *On Tartan Day 2002 nearly 8000 musicians took part in New York's Tunes of Glory parade on 6th Avenue.*

chosen because it marked the anniversary of the Declaration of Arbroath, which was signed on 6 April 1320. In effect, this was Scotland's declaration of independence, which Robert the Bruce and his followers sent to Pope John XXII, asserting their right to be free of the "yoke of English domination". It ended with the memorable sentiment: "For it is not for glory, riches or honour that we fight, but for freedom alone, that which no man of worth yields up, save with his life." The Arbroath document holds a particular resonance for all Americans, since their own Declaration of Independence was modelled on it. It is significant, too, that nearly half of the signatories on the American declaration had Scottish roots while, out of the 13 original United States, 9 had governors with Scottish ancestry.

Since its inception, there have been Tartan Day celebrations in Washington, New York, Boston and Chicago, and it seems certain that other cities will copy

this example. The tone of the festivities is similar to those of St Patrick's Day. In particular, the focal point of the event is usually a spectacular parade.

SCOTTISH PARLIAMENT

Tartan Day is not celebrated in the same way within Scotland, but politicians have been swift to recognize its value as a means of creating closer ties across the Atlantic. In 2003, Sir David Steel commented: "Tartan Day is hugely important... It captures the essence of the special links enjoyed by Scotland, Canada and America. I have no doubt Tartan Day...will reinforce this and help us gain a deeper mutual understanding."

In Scotland itself, the most important event of recent years has been the restoration of a Scottish parliament, after a gap of almost 300 years. This has done much to instil a renewed sense of national pride and confidence, which in turn has boosted the image of tartan. At the opening ceremony in 1999, the Queen wore a sample of a modern tartan – the Isle of Skye design. Shortly afterwards, a Scottish Parliament tartan came on the market, and this can now be purchased on a wide range of products – from braces to earrings. There could be no clearer sign that tartan is still flourishing, and will doubtless continue to do so for the foreseeable future.

▼ *The new Scottish parliament was officially opened in July 1999, in the presence of Queen Elizabeth.*

ACKNOWLEDGEMENTS

The publishers wish to thank the following agencies for supplying images for the book:

Aberdeen Art Gallery & Museums Collections: p25 *Baptism in Scotland* by John Phillip,

AKG (London): pp 28t Anglo Saxon manuscript illumination, 35t John Knox, unsigned engraving, 42 *The Celebrated Battle of Culloden* by Grainger, 57 *Ossian's Dream* by Jean-Auguste-Dominique Ingres, 1813, 60 *The Arrival of George IV at Leith Harbour* by Thomas Butterworth, 62 *Sir Walter Scott* engraving by William Walker after painting by Henry Raeburn, 63t *Jeanie Deans and Queen Caroline* by Charles Robert Leslie, 72t, 85t *American War of Independence Advance of the American Troops* by Francois Godefroy, 104b *Capt Robert Gray's Ship "Columbia"* by Louis Dodd, 120b, 121t,

Alamy Images: p50b.

The Bridgeman Art Library: p 1 *Four Gentlemen in Highland Dress* by Kenneth Macleay, 13 *Sir Mungo Murray* by John Michael Wright c1683, *Caledonians, or Picts*, engraving, English School 19th cent., 15t *Niel Gow* by Henry Raeburn, 1787, 24 *For Better of Worse – Rob Roy and the Baillie* by John Nicol, 1886, 28b *Mr Macready as Macbeth*, English School, 19th cent., 30bl *Robert the Bruce* from Seton's Armorial Crests, br *Baliol Doing Homage*, engraving, English School, 19th cent., 31b *The Death of John Comyn* by Felix Philippoteaux, 34b *Mary, Queen of Scots being led to Execution* by John Laslett Pott, 35b *James James VI of Scotland*, anon, 36t *The Beheading of King Charles I*, engraving, Dutch School, 1649, 38t *Kenneth Sutherland, 3rd Lord Duffus* by Richard Waitt, 38b *Portrait of a Jacobite Lady* by Cosmo Alexander, 42t *Prince Charles Edward Stuart Entering Edinburgh* by Thomas Duncan, 43l *Prince Charles at Holyrood, 1833* by William Simson, 43r *Bonnie Prince Charlie in Hiding after the Battle of Culloden*, English School, 19th cent., 45t *Flora Macdonald, 1747* by Richard Wilson, 46b *After Culloden: Rebel Hunting* by John Seymour Lucas, 51t *Lochaber No More, 1883* by John Watson Nicol, 54 *Distraining for Rent* by Sir David Wilkie, 1815, 55b *The Last of the Clan* by Thomas Faed, 61b *The Entry of George IV into Edinburgh* by John Ewbank, 1822, 64t *George IV in Highland Dress* by Sir David Wilkie, 1830, 65 *Colonel Alistair Macdonell of Glengarry* by Henry Raeburn, 1812, 67b *Deer Stalking in the Highlands* by Sir Edwin Landseer, 74t *The Order of Release* by Sir John Everett Millais, 1853, 74b *The MacNab* by Henry Raeburn, 75 *The Highland Shepherd* by Rosa Bonheur, 77 *Scottish Settlers in North America* by Thomas Faed, 81tl *Gustavus Adolphus II*, German School, 19th cent., 84 *A Soldier of the 79th highlanders at Chobham Camp in 1853* by Eugene-Louis Lamb, 87 *Sir John Sinclair* by Henry Raeburn, 92b *Caesar Crossing the Rubicon*, French School, 15th century, 93t *Anecdote of the Bravery of the Scottish Piper* by Franz Joseph Manskirch, *A Military Review* by John Wilson Ewbank.

Corbis: 83t.

Fine Art Photographic: front cover t & b, back cover t.

Getty Images: p76.

Historic Scotland: p23 (all).

Scotland In Focus: pp 2, 3, 4 (all), 7b, 8–9 & 19, 10, 11 (all), 12mr &b, 15b, 17b, 18, 19 (all), 20 (all), 21b, 26t, 26b courtesy of D Corrance, 27t, 29 (all), 32–33 & 40b, 36b, 39t, 44b, 45b, 46t, 49br, 52–53 & 66t, 55t, 69bl, bm & br, 70br, 71t, 78–79, 81b courtesy of The Strathnaver Museum, 85b, 88t courtesy of the Stirling Museum, 94–95 & 102, 100t, 101tr &b, 105m, 106, 114 (all), 120t, 122 (all) & 123 courtesy of the Jakarta Highland Games Society, 125t. All tartan samples in the book were also supplied by Scotland in Focus.

Scottish Viewpoint: p61t.

Mary Evans Picture Library: pp 22, 37, 41, 49bl, 50t, 56b, 58, 59bl & br, 63b, 73t & b,105tr.

National Library of Scotland: p34t, 40t, 68, 69t, 96 (all).

©The Trustees of the National Museums of Scotland: pp 5t, 12t, 16 (all), 17t, 27b, 64b, 66b, 67t, 86, 89b, 90, 91 (all), 93b, 97t, 100bl & br, 101tl, 109tl, 112t & b.

Peter Newark's Military Pictures: pp 31t, 48, 56t, 82.

www.PerfectPhoto.CA/©Rob Van Nostrand: pp 49t, 51b.

The Royal Bank of Scotland: p47.

St Andrews Links www.standrews.org.uk: p116.

Topham Picture Library: p69bl, 80bl, 81tr, 97t, 98, 119bl, 121b, 124 (all), 125b. Vinmag: 71b, 83b, 118 (all), 119t.

INDEX

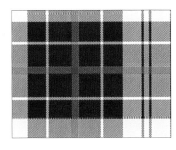

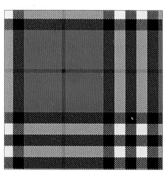